Alphonso Davies

A New Hope

Farhan Devji

Published by ECW Press
665 Gerrard Street East
Toronto, Ontario, Canada M4M 1Y2
416-694-3348 / info@ecwpress.com

Editor for the press: Michael Holmes
Substantive editor: Peter Norman
Cover design: Jessica Albert
Cover photograph: David Chant © Canada Soccer

This book is not authorized by or affiliated with
Alphonso Davies, Canada Soccer, FC Bayern
Munich, Vancouver Whitecaps FC, or any other
persons, organizations, or entities upon which
it reports.

A portion of each sale will be donated to UNHCR
Canada, supporting refugees in the world's most
vulnerable countries.

LIBRARY AND ARCHIVES CANADA CATALOGUING
IN PUBLICATION

Title: Alphonso Davies : a new hope /
Farhan Devji.

Names: Devji, Farhan, author.

Identifiers: Canadiana (print) 20220482896
| Canadiana (ebook) 20220482993

ISBN 978-1-77041-652-9 (softcover)
ISBN 978-1-77852-135-5 (ePub)
ISBN 978-1-77852-136-2 (PDF)
ISBN 978-1-77852-137-9 (Kindle)

Subjects: LCSH: Davies, Alphonso. | LCSH:
Soccer players—Canada—Biography. |
LCSH: Refugees—Canada—Biography. |
LCGFT: Biographies.

Classification: LCC GV942.7.D38 D48 2023
| DDC 796.334092—dc23

This book is funded in part by the Government of Canada. Ce livre est financé en partie par le gouvernement du Canada. We also acknowl-
edge the support of the Government of Ontario through the Ontario Book Publishing Tax Credit, and through Ontario Creates.

ONTARIO CREATES

Canadä

PRINTED AND BOUND IN CANADA

PRINTING: FRIESENS   5 4 3 2 1

MIX
Paper from
responsible sources
FSC
www.fsc.org   FSC® C016245

"This one's for everyone who's chasing a dream right now."

— Alphonso Davies, on Twitter,
after winning the UEFA Champions League on August 23, 2020

Contents

INTRODUCTION

I remember the first time I spoke to Alphonso Davies.

It was before he became the face of Canadian men's soccer and a beacon of hope for the national team. It was before his inspiring story was plastered across TV, phone, and computer screens world-wide. It was before he made a multi-million-dollar move to one of the biggest soccer clubs on the planet.

It was before *all* the fame.

Davies, then a member of the youth academy for Major League Soccer (MLS) club Vancouver Whitecaps FC, had just turned 15 a few months prior. No one outside his family, friends, and a very small circle in the Canadian soccer community would have even known his name. And if you ask any single one of them, many of whom you'll hear from throughout this book, they'll tell you the same thing: he's mostly the same person now as he was back then. Only with a bigger trophy case, a thicker wallet, and a few more million social media followers.

As we sat down in the lobby of a grandiose hotel in Tucson, Arizona (of all places), where the Whitecaps had convened for a training camp in February 2016, it became clear that Davies was still just a kid. He was polite and well-mannered, but his answers were brief, he was reluctant to maintain eye contact, and he mumbled his words at times. Before I arrived, and after I departed, Davies was fixated on his phone, instead of the picturesque desert mountains that surrounded us.

But this wasn't just *any* kid.

Rather, the picture of a grounded individual with a deep appreciation for his upbringing — and the opportunity in front of him — started to emerge. During that interview, Davies shared some of the hardships his parents had to endure so he could have a better life.

"Where we were living before, there were no opportunities for me and my family to be something," he said matter-of-factly.

The details of their past, at least as he knew them at the time, were murky. It's not something they spoke about often. But the underlying message, which Davies summed up perfectly when we broached the topic again a year later, was crystal clear.

"Stay humble at all times," he said when asked about the values his parents instilled in him. "You don't want to get carried away in anything you do. Stay humble, keep your feet on the ground. You came from nothing and you're coming to something, so you have to keep that mindset going."

These very words provide the backdrop for what MLS commissioner Don Garber once described to me as "one of the great soccer stories in the world."

It's the honour of my career to tell this story.

CHAPTER 1:
REFUGEE BABY

"Phonzie! Phonzie! Phonzie!"

The chants of his nickname reverberated across the stadium and around the world.

They were certainly heard at the Buduburam refugee camp, where amongst the embers of war a boy named Alphonso Davies was born at the turn of the century. Where those who remained saw him as a "shining light" that emerged from three decades of darkness.

They were heard from coast to coast in Canada, the country that gave Davies and his family a second chance at life.

And they were heard in Europe — this was the UEFA Champions League, after all.

Most of the home crowd had already departed. But a diehard contingent of travelling Bayern Munich supporters stayed back to send off their team, who had just beaten English Premier League giants Chelsea 3–0, and to serenade their reluctant superstar.

Davies wasn't quite sure how to react.

As ever, he was grinning from ear to ear. On this brisk Tuesday night at Stamford Bridge, an iconic football stadium in West London, his smile was even wider than usual. And that's saying something. Davies had just played the biggest match of his young career. Against the team he'd grown up watching on TV with his dad in their Northside Edmonton apartment.

He was, quite literally, living his dream.

At the same time, Davies was always taught to stay humble and keep his head down — he has his mom to thank for that. So he began to walk off the pitch with his teammates.

He didn't get very far.

Bayern's megastar striker Robert Lewandowski gently pushed him back towards the singing supporters.

This was Phonzie's moment.

Just minutes earlier, the 19-year-old had sent shockwaves across the soccer world with a jaw-dropping assist that affirmed his claim as one of the game's brightest young stars.

It started as a routine play.

Davies received the ball a few yards before the halfway line, where he was hugging the left touchline as he so often does. Instinctively, he positioned his body towards the opposition goal as he caressed the pass from a teammate and took a clean first touch.

That's when he saw it.

After a quick pass to Philippe Coutinho in midfield, Davies was off to the races. A trio of Chelsea players formed a triangle around him, but Davies accelerated right through the middle and picked up the bouncing loose ball that had been left behind. Now in full flight, he cleverly flicked the ball up past a sliding fourth Chelsea defender, leaving an awkward trail of disoriented bodies in his dust.

The crowd rose to its feet as Davies attacked the open space. They had just witnessed something special. And it wasn't over yet. Finally, Davies capped off his blistering run with an inch-perfect pass across the face of goal to Lewandowski, who tapped it home at the back post.

All this in a mere 10 seconds.

In those 10 seconds, Davies wasn't just a soccer player. He was an artist.

And this was his masterpiece.

As the ball hit the back of the net, Lewandowski — one of the greatest goalscorers of the generation — immediately turned back and pointed at Davies in awe. As did Thomas Müller. That's World Cup winner Thomas Müller.

The entire team swarmed him in front of the away supporters' section.

The kid they call Phonzie had arrived.

Alphonso Boyle Davies was born on November 2, 2000, in Gomoa Buduburam, as it's stated on his birth certificate, in the West African nation of Ghana. But his true origins can be traced a little further along the coast to the diminutive country known for being Africa's first independent republic.

That country is Liberia, whose unique history helps explain the events that would greatly impact the lives of Davies, his family, and so many of their compatriots.

Some more gravely than others.

In the late 1800s and early 1900s, most of Africa was colonized by European powers during the Scramble for Africa. Not little Liberia. It's one of the few countries in the world that never fell under European dominance.

That's because they already had a "big brother," as many saw it.

Look no further than their national flag. Alternating red and white horizontal stripes. A blue square in the top left corner bearing a white star. It's a near clone to the stars and stripes of the United States of America, representing the close ties between the two nations.

In 1816, a group of elite white men living in the U.S. founded the American Colonization Society (ACS), which eventually led to the creation of the country now known as Liberia.

The motives of the ACS were a point of contention from the very beginning.

Some claimed its goal was simply to end slavery in the U.S., which was still legal in certain states, and to help formerly enslaved Black people resettle in Africa. Others believed there was an implicitly racist nature to the organization, born out of a fear that a rising population of freed Black people would serve as a detriment to white America.

Regardless, the ACS proceeded with its plan and purchased a stretch of land along Africa's western shoreline, which became home to thousands of African Americans who migrated from the U.S. — some by choice, others by coercion.

And this was the basis upon which Liberia, meaning "Land of the Free," was formed.

Sadly, it never truly lived up to its name.

After remaining under the control of the ACS during its formative years, Liberia would declare independence in 1847. There were still significant American influences, however, including a constitution and flag resembling those of the U.S. And the first president of Liberia was U.S.-born Joseph Jenkins Roberts, who had emigrated from Virginia. For 133 years, in fact, Liberia was ruled by settlers from the U.S. — known as the Americo-Liberians. And they had no regard for the more populous indigenous communities that originally occupied the region.

In other words, the oppressed became the oppressors.

Finally, in 1980, a Liberian named Samuel Doe led a bloody coup to defeat the existing government, and he became the country's first indigenous leader. But that wasn't the end of the violence.

It was just the beginning.

Doe is remembered by many as a dictator whose regime was marked by human rights abuses and corruption. In an attempt to overthrow him, a rebel group led by Liberian warlord Charles Taylor invaded the country from neighbouring Ivory Coast on Christmas Eve, 1989.

And so began one of the deadliest civil wars in African history.

Davies's father, Debeah, and mother, Victoria, are Liberian nationals who hail from Maryland County on the southeastern tip of the country. But they were living in the capital city of Monrovia, named after former American president James Monroe, when the war erupted.

"That's where the president was living," Debeah said. "They were coming for the president."

And they didn't care who got in the way.

Debeah said there were instances when he'd be walking along the street only to have someone shot and killed right behind him. Victoria recounted having to "cross over bodies to go and find food." The sound of gunshots, and the sight of brutality, would become all too common.

Once Doe was eventually captured, he had his clothes stripped away and his ears and fingers cut off in a torture session that was videotaped and broadcast widely. Later, his mutilated corpse was displayed on the streets, an act that only intensified the fighting.

It wasn't uncommon to see young children patrolling the streets, firing AK-47s, and large groups of soldiers huddled in the backs of pickup trucks. If not assault rifles, they carried machetes, grenades, or rocket launchers. A lot of them wore street clothes, with bandanas or backward hats. Others were shirtless or even fully naked. Some of the men wore wigs and dresses as an intimidation tactic.

Buildings were burning down. Streets were deserted or, worse, destroyed.

"It was really, really dangerous," Debeah said.

There would be two brutal bouts of civil war between 1989 and 2003, claiming the lives of hundreds of thousands of Liberians. And many of those affected were children. A documentary produced by VICE, titled *The Cannibal Warlords of Liberia*, described the 14-year conflict as "a post-apocalyptic Armageddon with child soldiers smoking heroin, cross-dressing cannibals, and systematic rape."

It sounds like a horror movie, but for many, it was reality.

"I saw everything," Debeah said. "It was hard, man . . . Every day, your life is at risk."

It came to a point where Debeah and Victoria figured the only way to survive in Liberia was to literally fight for their lives. But that's not the life they wanted.

Not for themselves, and certainly not for their family.

"We didn't have any interest in shooting guns," Debeah said. "So we decided to just escape from there."

Amongst the cluster of small signs that appear just off the Accra–Cape Coast highway in Ghana is one that reads "Liberian Refugee Camp." In between the big red letters, there's a flag of Liberia on one side and a flag of Ghana on the other. At the bottom, a black arrow points towards the entrance of the camp.

If it wasn't for the sign, the camp might be mistaken for any other Ghanaian village.

A massive dirt soccer field can be seen from the main road. It's hard to miss. Not only is this where the real ballers play, it's also one of the largest gathering spots on the camp.

Opposite to the field, there are parked taxis, buses, and usually a few Toyota Land Cruisers belonging to staffers from the United Nations High Commissioner for Refugees (UNHCR), a UN agency dedicated to helping refugees, forcibly displaced communities, and stateless people.

Beyond the entrance, a labyrinth of unpaved roads leads into the different "zones" of the camp, which the residents first knew as "areas" associated with specific letters.

There are kids everywhere. Some are wearing uniforms, headed to school. Others are naked, bathing in plain sight outside their homes. Some are running around kicking soccer balls, seemingly without a worry in the world. Others are pushing wheelbarrows or carrying gallons of water on their heads, feeling the weight of the world on their shoulders.

Music is blaring. Women are going around selling fruits, vegetables, and other food. There are markets. There are restaurants/bars, or "chop bars," as the residents call them. There are barbershops, banks, internet cafes, and churches. Lots of churches.

There's celebration. There's laughter. There's life.

The people here are mostly Liberians. But this isn't war-torn Liberia.

This is Buduburam.

In 1990, the UNHCR helped the Ghanaian government establish the Buduburam refugee camp to house Liberians who had fled the war. It was the largest refugee camp in Ghana, at one point housing more than 40,000 Liberians.

And it was the unlikely birthplace for a future Canadian soccer star.

A 141-acre stretch of abandoned church land just west of Accra, Ghana's capital city, Buduburam looked a lot like other refugee camps when the first group of Liberians arrived. There were hundreds if not thousands of tents provided by the UNHCR, and not much else.

Over time, though, it developed into a lively, self-sufficient community. Many on the outside referred to it as a "model" refugee camp. The UNHCR and other aid organizations provided various forms of support, education, and training, but most of the businesses were built and run by the refugees. They found a way to make a life for themselves.

That's not to say life was easy.

There was nothing easy about it.

"It was very, very hard," Victoria said.

Buduburam resembled other impoverished villages in Ghana due to its dusty dirt roads and colourful makeshift shacks the refugees built from brick, clay, and whatever other materials they could scrounge together. Like many others, Debeah said, the family lived in a tent when they first arrived on the camp, before building a one-bedroom shack of their own.

Most of the homes would have been no bigger than 20 by 20 feet. They might have one or two rooms and, if you were lucky, a thin mattress to sleep on. Otherwise, it'd be a mat. In some homes, the women would lay down their lappas, traditional cloths a lot of Liberians wrapped around their bodies as garments, for the kids to sleep on.

None of the homes had proper bathrooms. Instead, there were a few "government toilets" or "toilet halls" scattered across the camp. These were communal wooden shacks with a handful of holes in the ground. People didn't like using them, because they were smelly, infested with flies, and poorly maintained. And a lot of people *couldn't* use them, because they were pay-per-use. So they preferred to do their business in the nearby "bush" or "gulf," as they called the forest area on the outskirts of the camp.

In the bush, people would encounter all sorts of wildlife. Snakes. Wildcats. Monkeys. And sometimes they'd encounter hostile strangers from nearby villages or the town of Kasoa.

Generally, though, during the day, people felt relatively safe in Buduburam.

Not so much at night.

There was hardly any light on the camp. Unless there was a full moon or someone had a flashlight, it'd be pitch-black. Not to mention, the camp was extremely congested — it was never meant to hold as many people as it did — and there was hostility from some of the locals.

15

There was a police station near the entrance with a gate that needed to be lifted for vehicles to enter, but anyone could just walk in on either side of the gate or through the bush. Armed robberies and assaults were common. Residents and visitors interviewed noted that it wasn't unusual to see dead bodies lying around the camp at any given time.

All that said, the biggest challenge Debeah and Victoria faced in Buduburam wasn't the crime. It was finding food for their son.

"Hunger kills people on the camp too," Debeah said. "It's not only a war zone [that kills people]. On the camp, if there's no food, people die, right? . . . With us, we can drink water and sleep, but he couldn't make it. So every day, we needed to make sure we found something for him to eat and make it in life."

That was the responsibility Davies's parents carried on their shoulders. They weren't worried about raising a soccer star. They were worried about keeping him alive.

"We were going to survive, for him," Debeah said. "We were going to find food, for him."

At first, the UNHCR and its partners provided water and food rations. Camp residents would line up at the food distribution centre for things like cocodolos and buckwheat, which people saw as cheaper variations of porridge and rice, as well as luncheon meats and cooking oil. But most of that had stopped by 2000, the same year Davies was born, due to a lack of funding and a regional policy to encourage Liberian refugees to return home after the first war, according to UNHCR reports.

Liberia was deemed to have undergone a credible election in 1997. It was an election, however, that saw Taylor transition from warlord to president after campaigning on the slogan "He killed my ma, he killed my pa, but I will vote for him."

Clearly, it was still a period of great peril. People were scared to go back.

So a lot of them stayed and were left to fend for themselves.

It was especially difficult for Debeah and Victoria, who were trying to raise Alphonso with hardly any money. And on the camp, pretty much everything came at a cost.

"We had to struggle by all means to get him going," Debeah said.

Debeah would sell ice blocks and perform construction work, earning just enough money to bring home some food and water. The staple food in Buduburam, as in many parts of Africa, was rice — accompanied by various sauces made from cassava leaves, potato leaves, and palm nuts, for example. People also ate traditional West African dishes such as peppersoup, a spicy soup with some sort of meat, alongside a white dough-like side called fufu. It's not that there wasn't any food around. It's just that not everyone could afford it.

For a lot of families, eating once per day was the norm.

"He always had something to eat, even when it wasn't enough, but at least to keep the system going," Debeah said.

Accessing clean drinking water was also a challenge. So residents arranged for water to be delivered from nearby Ghanaian towns. It was then stored on the camp in reservoirs or big black PolyTanks and sold by the bucket. Purified drinking water, "pure wata" or "mineral water" as the Liberians called it, was also sold in small plastic sachets that littered the camp. Those who couldn't afford these options had no choice but to fetch dirty water from ponds and wells a few hours away.

In 2005, the Buduburam camp failed to meet minimum standards for both available drinking water and sanitization, according to the UNHCR's Global Report that year. Water-borne illnesses were common. As were other diseases, such as malaria.

At night, people would get eaten alive by mosquitoes. Not everyone had proper windows or mosquito nets, and not everyone could afford malaria medication, so they'd rely on plants and other natural remedies from the bush.

Those worked sometimes. But not all the time.

There are a lot of reasons why Davies shouldn't have made it.

Although Davies was born during Liberia's darkest of days, it was also the height of soccer's popularity in the country. And this was the backdrop to his first introduction to the sport. It wasn't a formal introduction, by any means. And he has no memories of it to this day.

But it was an introduction, nonetheless.

"He kicked a ball in the back alley, in the yard," Debeah said.

17

"Between houses," Victoria added.

"In Africa, we call it football," Debeah continued, noting that he played for his school and club teams growing up. "Every kid, you gotta kick the ball."

There was a particular interest in football amongst Liberians during that time because of a man named George Weah, who is regarded as one of the greatest African players of all time. Debeah followed Weah's career closely and even used to watch his games and practices in person when the Monrovia-born striker was starting out in Liberia's domestic leagues.

"I used to watch him every day, every time, every practice," Debeah said. "We always used to go. Even if I didn't have transportation, I had to walk to go watch their club practising."

After short stints in Liberia, Ivory Coast, and Cameroon, the turning point in Weah's career came in 1988, when Cameroonian national team coach Claude Le Roy alerted Arsène Wenger to Weah's potential.

Today, Wenger is known as one of the most successful coaches in the history of the English Premier League, having won three league titles and seven FA Cups during a 22-year spell as head coach of Arsenal FC. At the time, though, he was the manager of AS Monaco — one of the biggest clubs in the French football leagues.

Wenger liked what he saw from Weah, who was in his early 20s, and brought him to Monaco for the Liberian's first footballing exploits outside of Africa.

He didn't disappoint.

Weah would go on to spend four years at Monaco, scoring 66 goals. He also enjoyed highly successful stints with European giants Paris Saint-Germain and AC Milan.

Known for his athleticism, dribbling, and finishing abilities, Weah established himself as one of the most prolific goalscorers of his generation and in 1995 became the first — and, to date, only — African to win the FIFA World Player of the Year and Ballon d'Or awards.

If that's not impressive enough, he's also remembered for scoring one of the greatest goals in the history of the game.

It was September 8, 1996. Matchday 1 of the Serie A campaign.

AC Milan vs. Hellas Verona FC.

Trailing 2–1 in the 85th minute, Verona were awarded an attacking corner. But they overhit it. The ball landed at Weah's feet beyond the back post. With a stylish first touch, he was off to the races. Weah picked up steam in midfield. He cruised by one defender. Then another. Spun past a third and fourth. Jumped around a fifth. With no fewer than five Verona players chasing him, Weah accelerated into the attacking box and fired a low right-footed strike into the bottom left corner to complete the sensational solo effort.

It's a sight to see. Seriously, just YouTube it.

Although he made a name for himself at the club level, Weah also represented the Liberian national team. He led Liberia to their only two appearances in the Africa Cup of Nations, in 1996 and 2002, and brought them to within a single point of the 2002 FIFA World Cup, the closest they've ever come to qualifying.

Whenever Liberia played, people in Buduburam would gather around small TVs in the camp's videoclubs to watch the games. For a fee, of course. A few times, Weah travelled to the camp to visit the Liberians, resulting in absolute pandemonium. There were huge crowds. There was looting. People couldn't contain their excitement.

Everyone wanted to see "King George."

"He was like the pope to us," one resident explained.

The height of Weah's soccer career coincided almost precisely with the civil wars in his native land, providing a little bit of joy for Liberians during an otherwise turbulent time.

"I had to do what I had to do," Weah told *The Guardian*. "I decided to be strong and play to better the negative image of my country. People were very devastated at home and I could never forget about my country but for just 90 minutes I could make that sacrifice and do it."

In a way, Weah helped unite a country that was broken. And that is something he would strive to do again years later — this time, in a more official capacity.

Weah was sworn in as the 25th president of Liberia in January 2018, vowing to tackle corruption, boost the economy, promote human rights, and improve living conditions in a country that is still one of the poorest in the world. Weah's election was particularly notable because it marked Liberia's first peaceful transfer of power between democratically elected leaders in more than 70 years. Finally, it would appear, hope had been restored.

For Davies and his family, however, hope came in a different form.

CHAPTER 2:
BECOMING CANADIAN

A bright room adorned by wooden panels, floor-to-ceiling windows, and two drooping Canadian flags behind the stage awaited Davies as he took the test. The room was simple and small enough not to feel extravagant, yet elegant enough to mark the occasion.

And what an occasion it was.

Both Vancouver Whitecaps FC and Canada Soccer had videographers on site. The Whitecaps were set to release a documentary about his family's journey, titled *Becoming Canadian: The Alphonso Davies Story*. Canada Soccer was ready to announce his first call-up to the senior men's national team and get him on a plane to join their camp in Montreal.

The president of Canada Soccer was even standing by, eager to present the budding 16-year-old superstar with a Canadian national team jersey crested with "Davies" on the back.

Davies just had to pass his citizenship test.

No pressure, kid.

As he so often does — be it on a soccer pitch or, in this case, tucked away in a downtown Vancouver commercial building that houses Canada's local citizenship office — Davies passed with flying colours: 19 out of 20.

And just like that, he became a Canadian citizen.

Well, almost.

Donning an unassuming white T-shirt and blue jeans, accompanied by a lanyard dangling out of his pocket, Davies entered the ceremony room where the Oath of Citizenship would take place. It was mostly full of fellow citizens-to-be at that point. He quietly slipped past a few of them, picked up the miniature Canadian flag that had been left on his seat, and waved it around with a goofy smile on his face. Because, of course, he did.

The citizenship ceremony would begin moments later, with the presiding official specifically calling out Davies in his opening remarks.

"I don't usually pay note to any particular person in this ceremony," he said from the podium, "but you should know that we're privileged to have, from Ghana, a member of the Vancouver Whitecaps . . . who will play on the Canadian national team, which is a wonderful thing as a newly minted Canadian citizen. So I want to pay special welcome to Alphonso Davies."

Davies briefly stood up and acknowledged the applause that ensued. There was that goofy smile again.

The rest of the ceremony was like any other.

Together with their right arms raised, Davies and his fellow countrymates recited the Oath of Citizenship — once in English and once in French, the country's two official languages — before receiving their citizenship certificates and singing the national anthem.

Now it was official.

"Not many people can say they're a Canadian citizen, knowing that it's one of the best countries in the world," Davies said in a Whitecaps press release distributed later that day. "I'm very proud that I'm one of those people."

Two lineups quickly formed following the proceedings. In one of them, some of the new Canadians posed for photos with the presiding official. In the other, some of the staffers posed for photos with Davies.

There was a busy day ahead of him. He had some promotional photos and interviews to get out of the way. He had an appointment scheduled to get braces on his teeth. And he had to pack for the trip to Montreal, where he would join the senior national team for the first time.

But first, as he recounted to BBC's *Football Focus*, a phone call to Mom was in order.

"I'm so happy for you," he remembered her saying.

"Yeah, Mom. I got it. I'm a citizen of Canada!"

His parents couldn't be there with him. But they were certainly on his mind. Earlier that day, Davies sat alone in a quiet hallway, hunched over, watching the Whitecaps' yet-to-be-released documentary on a phone as he waited for the ceremony to begin.

It was the first time he learned the gruesome details of his parents' time in Liberia during the war. They'd never discussed it with him as a kid. Not like that, at least. It was the first time he heard his parents speak so candidly about the struggles of living, and raising a child, in a refugee camp. It was the first time he saw his mom cry.

This day wasn't for the Whitecaps or Canada Soccer.

It was for Mom and Dad.

"This was something my parents went through but they didn't make it," he told Canada Soccer that day. "I'm glad that I could do it for them and do it for the family."

Living in a refugee camp is meant to be a temporary measure.

For that reason, the UNHCR promotes three "durable solutions" to help refugees rejoin society. There's voluntary repatriation, in which the refugee returns to their country of origin — in this case, Liberia. There's local integration, in which the refugee is granted the permanent right to remain in the country of asylum: Ghana. And there's resettlement, in which the refugee starts a new life in a third country.

Although the war had ended, returning to the ravaged nation of Liberia was still not considered an optimal solution in the early to mid-2000s, due to the poor living conditions and unstable political, social, and economic climate. And there was a reluctance from both parties, as well as a host of logistical challenges, for Liberian refugees to permanently settle in Ghana.

For many, that left resettlement as the most desirable option.

Ultimately, though, it was up to the UNHCR to rule on each resettlement claim based on the refugee's vulnerability — and, of course, to the third country to accept them.

"Pretty much how it worked, the UNHCR would be petitioning governments to resettle as many refugees as they can," said Krista Zongolowicz, a former UNHCR resettlement officer who worked in Buduburam at the time. "When we'd have governments coming in to look at Buduburam camp to see if they'd be interested in resettling refugees from there, we'd be escorting the government officials, taking them out on trips to see the life out there, and trying to help them understand why this is not a long-term situation."

The UNHCR would post the names of those accepted for resettlement on bulletin boards across the Buduburam camp, including one just outside the yellow multi-storey building in Area T that residents knew as the "mansion." People would desperately hope and pray for their names to appear. Sometimes, they'd spend hours combing through the list, only to realize their names weren't there.

"It was the hub for excitement and sadness as well," one resident recalled. "That could make or break you."

The grim reality, according to the UNHCR, is that less than 1 percent of the world's refugees are resettled each year.

"Refugee life is like if they put you in a container and then they lock you up," Victoria said. "No way to get out."

She wasn't speaking literally, but it's how a lot of them felt.

In 2006, only 1,221 refugees living in Ghana — mainly Liberians — were resettled through the UNHCR's programs, as per the UNHCR resettlement data finder. Among them, 784 landed in the United States, 332 in Australia, 103 in Canada, and 2 in the Netherlands.

Fortunately, Davies and his parents were among the lucky few.

The U.S. was typically seen as the most attractive destination for Liberian refugees. Remember, there's a lot of history there. In Africa, Liberia was known as "Small America." Many Liberians still had family members in the U.S. who were sending over money to support them. Debeah said he had an uncle there, fighting for the family to come over.

That didn't work out. But another country stepped up.

"On the camp they had a camp commandant, where we go into the office and they bring you a file," Debeah recalled. "They said, 'OK, you fill in the form for Canada.' I said, 'Why?' I studied the history and whatsoever, but I didn't even know somebody in Canada here."

Not unlike the U.S., Canada has long been considered a land of immigration and one of the world leaders in accepting refugees. Nearly one in four people who live there were born outside of its borders. And just a few years earlier, in 2002, the Canadian government implemented the Immigration and Refugee Protection Act, which placed a greater emphasis on protecting refugees over their ability to successfully establish in the country. Notably, this came in the wake of the 9/11 terrorist attacks in the U.S., which saw refugee admissions drop significantly south of the border.

Canada isn't immune to the racism, xenophobia, and systemic discrimination that has plagued Black, Indigenous, and other people of colour for years. But Debeah and Victoria knew that it could offer a better life for their son, so they went ahead with the process. It was a lengthy one, usually starting with an interview at the UNHCR office in Buduburam.

"In this big hall, we'd set up tables, workstations, processing I don't know how many hundreds of people per day," Zongolowicz recalled, though she didn't have any specific recollection of the Davies family. "And then you bring in one family at a time, you have a conversation with them, you're probably at your own laptop, writing up all the kids' names, birthdates, asking the kid, 'Is this really your name? Is this really your mom?' Trying to ascertain whether there's any extra information that needs to go in their file."

Between interviews, health and security screening, and processing time, the resettlement process could take months, if not years, depending on the backlog of cases. One of the final steps was an orientation, where the refugees learned more about where exactly they were headed. In the case of Davies and his family, that was Windsor, Ontario.

"After the orientation they said, 'You're going to this province, you're going to this province, you're going to this province,'" Debeah recalled. "And that's how we got to Windsor."

Several factors are considered to determine a refugee's destination — whether they have any friends or family living in Canada, the availability of settlement services, the languages they speak, the ethnic, cultural, and religious communities in the area, and so on. Traditionally, the province of Ontario has been the most popular destination. And Windsor, the southernmost city in Canada, was one of the original cities in Ontario designated as an official landing spot for Canada's Government-Assisted Refugees.

Debeah and Victoria didn't have any connection to the region, however. Although it presented its challenges, Africa was all they knew. The only home they'd ever had. Now they were in a completely foreign land.

They had no family.

No friends.

Nothing.

Davies, who was five years old when the family immigrated, said he found it tough to make friends because he was shy and he didn't know the language well. Victoria said she felt homesick and had trouble sleeping. She and Debeah both struggled to find work. Initially, they relied on the government's financial support. But that was only available for the first year. From that point forward, they were on their own.

But after everything they'd been through, everything they'd sacrificed, they weren't about to let this opportunity slip away.

They *couldn't*.

About a year after they landed in Windsor, their journey took them 3,000 kilometres northwest, from Canada's southernmost city to its northernmost metropolis: Edmonton, Alberta. There, Debeah found work packing chicken at Maple Leaf Foods, a meat processing plant, and Victoria as a cleaner at the University of Alberta Health Centre.

Very quickly, Canada started to feel like home. And even more so when Davies's younger brother, Bryan, and then his sister, Angel, were born. Their kids were safe. They were making just enough to put food on the table. And Davies started going to school.

It wasn't a lot, but this was *everything* Debeah and Victoria had ever wanted.

"If I look back, where we came from, refugee camp, no food, no clothes, and here we are today," Victoria said in 2017, fighting back tears. "He has everything that he needs."

Like many Canadian friendships, this one started with a game of street hockey.

Chernoh Fahnbulleh, who grew up in Liberia before immigrating to Canada in 2008, used to visit his grandmother every week at her apartment just outside downtown Edmonton.

Every so often, he'd see a young boy around his age playing outside. It was Davies, who lived in the same building with his parents. As time went on, they started to recognize each other. So they'd say "hi hi," Fahnbulleh recalled, and go on with their days.

Until that game of street hockey.

"From there, he came over to my grandma's house and then it just took off," Fahnbulleh said.

Neither of their families had much, but as Fahnbulleh said, they "made a lot with what [they] had." He and Davies loved playing different sports. And they loved going out to eat at Subway and KFC/Taco Bell, where they'd usually get the special: two tacos, a small fries, and a drink for around five dollars.

But there was nothing quite like Mom's cooking. Whenever Victoria asked what they wanted to eat, it was an easy answer. They didn't even have to think about it.

Jollof rice.

"That's probably our favourite," Fahnbulleh said of the famous West African dish. "It's just rice with a lot of vegetables and chicken."

Best of all, it was a little taste of home.

Davies grew up in what he calls a Liberian household — from the cuisine to the language and the traditional gospel music his mom played early every Sunday morning before they went to church. He wasn't as connected to Ghanaian culture, but Ghana was still his first home. Sometimes, he wore a wristband with red, gold, and green horizontal stripes and a big black star in honour of Ghana's national flag. At the same time, Davies very much felt Canadian.

27

That was a balancing act.

In those early days, Davies spoke Liberian English. Or, as he calls it, "broken English."

As Fahnbulleh recalled, there was one time they were hanging out with a big group of friends talking about where they should go eat when Davies suggested: "*Buhga* King."

"Huh?" someone responded.

"*Buhga* King," he repeated.

He meant Burger King, of course. But he just pronounced it with a thick accent, as was common in Liberian English. Certain words were also different altogether.

"Instead of saying, 'Oh, is that your girlfriend?' You'd say, 'Oh is that your jue?'" Fahnbulleh explained. "People would be like, 'Whaaat? What do you mean by that?'"

In those situations, everyone would typically have a laugh.

"I'd break it down to them and tell them what he meant by that," Fahnbulleh said. "It was just harder for them to understand the broken English."

That also made school a bit harder for Davies. He never went to school on the refugee camp — his parents couldn't afford it. So this was an entirely new experience.

In one class, the students had to read one page of a book aloud, in front of everyone, before passing it along to a classmate of their choice. Davies, Fahnbulleh, and their friends liked to put each other on the spot. They kept going in circles.

At some point, it always came back to Davies.

"He'd do a good job, but he'd just read it slow," Fahnbulleh recalled. "At the time, reading-wise, he was getting the basics of it. And we all knew that. For a lot of us, reading wasn't our best thing. We were always joking around with it. We didn't actually put each other down, saying 'You can't read, blah, blah, blah.' We knew we were all learning and we were all going to get there."

Davies was forced to attend a few different elementary schools in Edmonton. It's not that there were any problems — on one occasion, Debeah said, the principal called him and begged for Davies to stay because he was a track and field star. Rather, his parents had to move around town to find affordable housing.

28

They didn't have any other choice.

Eventually, they settled in a modest four-storey apartment building in Clareview, a residential area in Northeast Edmonton that many working-class families called home.

"His parents were very serious people," said Nedal Huoseh, one of Davies's youth soccer coaches, who would become a close family friend and advisor. "They gotta go out there and work, feed their family, and pay the bills. That was the focus."

Due to the nature of their jobs, Debeah and Victoria didn't work regular hours.

Sometimes, they both worked the night shift and had to sleep during the day. Debeah might start at 3 or 4 a.m. and come home in the afternoon, while Victoria might start at 10 p.m. and come home around 8 a.m. They couldn't afford a babysitter, either.

So a lot of the time, Davies was in charge at home.

Huoseh recalled picking up Davies at the apartment to drive him to soccer practice, only to have to wait an extra 10 or 15 minutes before he was ready to leave.

"I was thinking, Why can't he just come now?" Huoseh wondered at the time. "So I knocked on his door one day. I thought I'd just go up and check on him. I went up to the apartment, walked up, and I was like, 'Hey man, what's going on, you ready to go?'"

That's when Huoseh saw that Davies was alone with the kids.

He was in the middle of changing diapers.

"I can't leave yet," he remembered Davies saying. "My parents aren't here. I just have to take care of the kids until my dad gets here."

"Oh, OK, you're babysitting?"

"Yeah, this is how it is every day."

Davies's brother would have been three or four at the time. His sister was an infant.

There was a lot of responsibility on his shoulders.

"This kid's like 12 years old. Not even," Huoseh said. "I was thinking, Oh wow, that's very mature. That's the first time it kind of hit me. Like, wow, my 11-year-old doesn't even know what a diaper looks like anymore."

That type of thing is relatively normal in the African community, according to Fahnbulleh. Every once in a while, he'd come over and hang out with Davies while he was taking care of the kids. He remembers Davies having to walk over to the Clareview Walmart to grab food and other supplies. He also remembers the time they made peppersoup together.

"It was mostly just soup and fish," Fahnbulleh said. "The way our parents made it, it didn't taste the same, but we had to come up with something and just make it for the little ones."

Fahnbulleh never once heard Davies complain about the situation. He knew it was part of his responsibility as a big brother. He knew his parents had to work.

It's just how it was.

"He was always there for them," Fahnbulleh said. "Whatever they needed."

Early family pictures reveal their special relationship.

In one photo, a young Davies has his hand on his brother's chin, encouraging a big smile. They are both grinning from ear to ear. In another, he's embracing his baby sister from behind — his arms wrapped around her waist — and looking down at her with admiration.

Davies isn't the oldest sibling — he's the third youngest of six — but it felt like he was because the others were still back in Africa. Years later, the family would be reunited with his older sister, Tutu. Born in Liberia, she was separated from the family amid the chaos of the war and unable to join them in Edmonton until Davies was a teenager.

"When I first saw her, I was like, 'This is kind of weird,'" Davies said in his YouTube vlog. "My own sister, living in the house, but in my mind she's a stranger to me."

But they quickly formed a special bond. Davies showered her infant daughter, his niece, with love the same way he did with his siblings. Only this time, he had a bit more experience.

For Debeah and Victoria, those moments serve as validation for the decision they made to start a new life in Canada. It's not the goals or trophies they cherish. It's their family being together. Food on the table. A roof over their heads. Education for their kids. Safety and security. And something as simple as the ability to earn a living.

"What I like about this country, if you're strong, you will make it in life," Debeah said. "If I go to work for one hour, at the end of two weeks, they will pay me for one hour. That's what I like about it. They won't say, 'OK, we don't have money to pay you.' Every time I go to work, after two weeks I get my pay every time. So everything is OK for me."

"With me, I like to be independent," Victoria added. "I like to do things on my own. I like the country. I like to work. Keep myself busy. Stay out of trouble . . . I just want to say thanks to the Canadian government because they brought us here. We had no family here. I appreciate it so much for my son and my family."

Davies is proud of where he came from. He'll never forget his African roots. But by his own admission, Canada is home.

His earliest memories are not from the refugee camp but from Windsor, where he experienced snow for the first time — waking up one morning, "seeing this white stuff lying on the ground," and going outside in shorts and a T-shirt to figure out what it was, as he recounted in an article for *The Players' Tribune*. And then, of course, there was the flight to Edmonton.

"I was so fascinated with the airplane that I wanted to be a pilot," he said.

He'll forever be grateful to the country for opening its doors. And he'll forever be grateful to his parents for carrying the family to a safe environment. They're his drive. They're his inspiration.

Everything he does is for them.

"Knowing that we fought so hard to come to a country like Canada, that we can be and do whatever we want," Davies said in 2016, "it's a big motivation to me."

CHAPTER 3:
THE BEAUTIFUL GAME

Edmonton is known for many things.

For starters, its location. The capital city of Alberta, one of three Canadian prairie provinces, Edmonton has been dubbed the "Gateway to the North" due to its proximity to Canada's northern communities and resources.

Its landscape. Encircled by a seemingly never-ending stretch of prairie grasslands, forests, and wheat fields, Edmonton features predominantly flat terrain and a winding river valley bisecting the city.

Its oil industry. Nicknamed the "Oil Capital of Canada," it's the closest major centre to Alberta's oil sands, which have one of the largest oil reserves in the world.

Its hockey team. The Oilers, as they're aptly named, are an immense source of pride and passion. In addition to winning five Stanley Cups, they've been blessed with some of the greatest players of all time, including "The Great One" himself, Wayne Gretzky, and most recently Connor McDavid and Leon Draisaitl.

Its long and cold winters. We're talking temperatures as low as minus 40 degrees and snow on the ground for one-third of the year. Bring a parka.

Its mall. No, seriously, it has a *really* big mall.

One thing it's never been known for?

Soccer.

And yet it was in Edmonton that Davies fell in love with the beautiful game.

Amid a sea of residential neighbourhoods in Northside Edmonton's Dickinsfield community lies a green haven of grass fields, sitting adjacent to the rotunda-like structure that is Northmount Elementary School. Davies spent a lot of time on those fields as a young child, kicking a ball around at lunchtime and after school. His friends thought he was pretty good. So they invited him to join them for a tryout at Edmonton Internazionale Soccer Club, or Inter SC — a youth club in the area named after the world-famous Italian team.

Davies didn't have any soccer boots or shin pads, but that wasn't going to stop him. He showed up and played in his running shoes.

"I really impressed them," Davies said in one of his YouTube vlogs. "Then we're all sitting down talking, the coach came and said, 'I just want to say to everyone, you had a great tryout, and all of you are on the team.' I was like, 'Hold on, we *all* made the team?'"

Just like that, Davies began playing organized soccer. At nine years old, it was later than most kids had started, but it wouldn't take him long to get up to speed.

"People started telling me, 'Alphonso, if you keep working, you could become something,'" Davies recalled in 2016. "So I kept going at it."

Davies's situation was treated as a "hardship case" at Inter, according to his first coach, John Tadic. Knowing his parents were struggling financially, the club had them sign a templated letter requesting that his registration fees be waived.

And they were, every year he was there.

"I sat down with his parents, I went to his house, I saw the situation," Tadic said.

Most of his dealings with Davies's parents were at their low-income home in Boyle Street — an inner-city neighbourhood known for its homelessness and high crime rate. They were working multiple jobs. They rarely had the time to attend games. At most, Tadic said, he saw Debeah at the field a handful of times over a couple of years. Like his son, he always had a smile on his face.

After games, Tadic and his girlfriend would take Davies to the mall to grab a bite to eat at the food court. Sitting right across from him, they couldn't help but notice the state of his clothes.

"He had some old pants with holes in it and things like that," Tadic recalled. "My girlfriend made a comment to me, that she saw those clothes he was wearing and it made her want to cry."

So Tadic and some of the parents on the team helped Davies out with things like track pants, shorts, cleats, and shin pads. They also drove him to games and practices — on the way there, Davies loved listening to "I Wish" by Skee-Lo from Tadic's old CD mix. Meanwhile, a local charity named Sport Central donated soccer balls and his first bike, which Davies once said gave him the "sense of freedom" to get around himself.

"He was a great little player," Tadic said. "He just needed help."

Davies lived in the northern part of town for most of his child-hood. But the family's Boyle Street apartment sat on the outskirts of downtown, not far from Commonwealth Stadium, where Davies once snuck into a Canadian Football League Grey Cup game. And it was right across the street from Mother Teresa Catholic School, where he finished elementary school.

Through Mother Teresa, Davies was introduced to a free after-school soccer program called Free Footie. The program was designed to help underprivileged students without the means — financial or otherwise — to play soccer. Many of the participants were living in poverty. Many were immigrants and had similar stories to Davies's.

Marco Bossio, head of the soccer academy at St. Nicholas Catholic Junior High School in Northeast Edmonton, saw Davies play for the first time at a year-end Free Footie tournament. It wasn't an organized tournament, Bossio said, but more of a "free play type of thing" on the north bank of the river valley at Rundle Park.

Davies, who was 11 at the time, was running circles around the others. And much to Bossio's delight, he'd already signed up to join St. Nicholas the following school year.

"He came up to me with this big smile and said he's coming to our soccer academy," Bossio recalled. "You could see this passion for the game. He was super motivated right from the start."

For the next three years, Davies would spend his weekdays at St. Nicholas and then practise or play matches in the evenings and weekends with his new club, Edmonton Strikers.

It was the perfect combination.

At St. Nicholas, Davies was surrounded by like-minded individuals serious about pursuing a career in the game. Its in-house soccer academy was designed to keep kids engaged at school, while developing their skills both on and off the field through fitness and health programs, film sessions, and more.

With the Strikers, he was able to play in a competitive club soccer environment against the top talent in the city and in prestigious tournaments across North America. At the same time, there wasn't a ton of pressure on Davies. Unlike Inter, who won every single one of their games leading up to the provincials in Davies's final season, the Strikers weren't one of the best teams. They were one of the worst.

But they were a *team*.

It was through the Strikers that Davies was first introduced to Huoseh, or "Coach Nick." Davies was friends with Huoseh's son, who also moved from Inter to Strikers, so he followed suit. Huoseh was accused of stealing him. Tensions between the two clubs were high.

But in the end, the decision was left with Davies.

"I'm still not sure *why* I did it," he wrote in *The Players' Tribune*, "but I'm glad I did."

As Davies noted, Huoseh quickly became a "central part" of his life. His parents were doing everything they could, but for Davies to keep playing soccer at a high level, they knew they couldn't do it on their own.

So they turned to Huoseh.

"His dad said, 'Well, you know, you have to deal with everything, I don't have time, I work shift work, I can't really afford to put him into the sport,'" Huoseh recalled. "I said, 'That shouldn't be a problem.' I was already at that time looking after half a dozen boys that couldn't afford to play club league soccer. I said, 'OK, sure, add another one to the list.'"

Huoseh was more than a coach.

He was a mentor. A chauffeur. A "stepfather to Alphonso," as Debeah called him. Whenever Davies needed something, whether it was a ride to Cumberland Park for training on the other side of town, food on the table, or just some friendly words of advice, Huoseh was there.

"He cared about me as if I was his own," Davies wrote in *The Players' Tribune*.

As time went on, he became someone the family really trusted. Someone they could count on. And years later, when Davies needed an agent, they wanted him.

No one else.

To this day, Davies lists Huoseh as one of his biggest role models. And his parents credit Huoseh more than anyone else for their son's progression in the game. Not for teaching him the x's and o's per se, but for the constant support and guidance through the years.

"Nick comes second," Debeah said, "and God comes first."

Even back then, everyone could see that Davies had something.

Something special.

With the Strikers, he was usually deployed in the middle of the park as an attacking midfielder with the freedom to roam — he wore number 10, commonly reserved for the most creative or offensively gifted player on the team — or as a centre forward. With St. Nicholas, he was more of a right-sided forward. Wherever he was, the ball seemed to follow.

Davies had a lovely left foot. Great ball control. A big-time shot. But upon first glance, it was his athleticism that usually caught people's attention. Davies was faster than everyone else, including the older kids he played against.

Way faster.

"He was always a step ahead of everyone on the field," Huoseh said.

Sometimes two or three.

Part of it was pure speed, but he also saw things that others didn't.

That was certainly evident in one game Davies played with the Strikers at a tournament in Las Vegas, Nevada. With his teammate looking for options in midfield, Davies suddenly turned on the jets a few yards before the halfway line and blew by the entire opposition back line, creating a passing lane that wouldn't have otherwise existed. He then received the ball in full flight, fended off a defender, took two touches, and calmly finished with his favoured left foot. It was like he was in cruise control. A muted fist pump ensued, as if it was no big deal.

And for Davies, it wasn't. It happened all the time.

Heck, he had three goals and two assists in a game the day before, including an off-balance scissor-kick volley in which he flicked the ball up to himself in the box before firing it through the legs of the goalkeeper.

Unsurprisingly, Davies also excelled at track and field and cross-country running. Yes, he ran the 100-metre sprint, recording a personal best time between 11 and 12 seconds in junior high.

He was very good at basketball and volleyball too.

He even tried hockey, a rite of passage for Canadians. His friend's dad owned a skating rink, where Davies *attempted* to skate for the first time. The same friend was a big fan of Washington Capitals power forward Alexander Ovechkin, so Davies supported him, too, and had his own Ovechkin T-shirt.

But soccer always came first.

In the spring and early summer, he'd play outdoor soccer. In the fall and winter, when it'd be too cold and snowy outside, he'd mostly play in gymnasiums or indoor boarded facilities — essentially hockey rinks with artificial turf. Indoor soccer allows kids to play year-round in Edmonton, while also developing their technical skills by forcing them to control the ball in tighter spaces — one of Davies's finest traits.

In addition to his school soccer with St. Nicholas and club soccer with the Strikers, Davies was also part of the Alberta North provincial team during the winters. This team was made up of all the best players in the region, mostly from Edmonton. They had a big rivalry with the team from the south. Those games were usually close. But during tryouts one year, the north won 6–0.

Davies scored four of the goals.

"And they weren't, like, nice build-up plays," recalled Alberta North coach Sergio Teixeira. "He just took the ball and went right down their throats, every single time."

Teixeira noted that Davies could flip a switch and take over a game at any given moment. And he could do it in different ways.

"When he got pissed, he knew how to tackle," Teixeira said. "He's not a little Boy Scout on the field. He does have that mean streak. But that's what gave him a competitive edge."

The provincial team would train on Saturdays and Sundays inside the Commonwealth Fieldhouse, where "only the strong survive," as Davies once said. If there was ever a conflict with a player's club team games, Teixeira had a clear rule in place: don't come to training.

And yet?

"Alphonso didn't care what time the Strikers played at," Teixeira said. "If they played at noon, somehow he always showed up for that two o'clock session. Or if they played at four o'clock, he'd come to our session first and then go to a game. He did not want to miss it, ever."

He just loved the game.

On weekends, he and his dad would watch European soccer on TV. His dad supported Chelsea, thanks in part to players like Didier Drogba and Michael Essien, so they became Davies's team by default. Not only were Drogba and Essien two of Chelsea's most important players in the early 2000s, they're also among the greatest African footballers of all time. And there was a connection to both of them. Essien was born in Accra, about an hour away from Buduburam, and Drogba in Ivory Coast, a neighbouring country to Liberia.

Davies's favourite player, though, was Lionel Messi.

At St. Nicholas, Bossio would let his students watch UEFA Champions League matches on Tuesdays and Wednesdays. Because of the time difference, they'd kick off around lunchtime. Bossio projected the matches onto the whiteboard in his classroom, and the kids couldn't take their eyes off it. Davies liked watching all the games. But he especially liked watching Messi, who's one of the greatest to ever play the game. If not *the* greatest.

He and his friends often had the age-old debate: Messi vs. Ronaldo. Who's better? Over time, he gained an appreciation for both of their talents.

But back then, it was all Messi, all the time.

As a fellow left-footed attacker, Davies wanted to be just like him. Sometimes before his own matches, he'd even watch highlight videos of the Argentine to get himself pumped up.

"I like his playing style, his dribbling, passing, shooting, just everything about him," Davies said in 2018. "The way he carries himself on the field, he doesn't cry, he doesn't whine, he doesn't dive. He's just a great role model."

By the time he'd joined St. Nicholas in Grade 7, there was no doubt in Davies's mind what he wanted to do with his life. In fact, there's a video from that first year in which Bossio asks him, "What are your goals as a player?"

It's an exercise Bossio went through with each of his players early in the school year to learn more about them and help get them out of their comfort zone.

Swimming in an oversized jersey that he was forced to tuck in during games, a baby-faced and somewhat jittery Davies responded, "My goal as a player is to reach the professional level and probably play with some of the pros."

"I remember everyone else in the room laughing at him. Just like, 'Nah, what is this kid talking about?'" said Gloire Amanda, the team's best player before Davies arrived. "But the way he said it, to me, he looked like he meant it."

Amanda described Davies as a "small, short, and skinny" kid when he first came to the school. As a Grade 7 student playing with and against students who were mostly in Grades 8 and 9, he was a full head shorter than a lot of people on the field.

"When you first look at him, you wouldn't think that this kid can hurt you in a game," Amanda said.

Until they saw him with a ball at his feet.

St. Nicholas won the city championship in each of the three years Davies was there. One of the best goals he scored came against Cardinal Léger on a beautiful autumn day in Northeast Edmonton. It was one of his very first goals, and games, at the school.

And it's still talked about to this day.

With the amber-toned foliage providing the backdrop for St. Nicholas's lush green fields, Davies leaned into a bouncing loose ball outside the 18-yard box and powered a perfectly executed half volley into the top corner.

Everyone's jaws collectively dropped. Like, visibly. Davies's teammate closest to the goal placed his hands on his head as he turned back to him. Another simply covered his mouth.

"I'll never forget that moment," Amanda said. "It was like, 'What did he just do?'"

"A lot of the parents, other coaches, and some of the teachers on staff that were watching this game couldn't believe that a Grade 7 student just did that," Bossio added. "It was pretty remarkable."

Then there was the goal against St. Elizabeth Seton.

"It's coming there, you know it's coming!" the opposing coach yelled as Davies received a lofted pass.

And yet there was nothing they could do to stop him.

With his first touch, Davies headed the ball over the first defender that approached him. It landed perfectly at his feet. As he cut to the middle of the pitch from the right, a pair of opposing players lunged at him one by one. But Davies skipped past each of them. With his momentum now carrying him away from the goal, Davies finally released an off-balance left-footed strike back the other direction and into the bottom right corner of the net.

"When I saw that goal, I looked over to my assistant coach and said, 'I think we're looking at a young Arjen Robben,'" Bossio said, referencing the longtime Bayern Munich winger — and Davies's future teammate — famously known for cutting inside from the right to score goals with his left foot.

After both goals, Davies jumped into Amanda's arms in celebration.

Amanda was a few years older than Davies and already drawing interest from professional clubs FC Edmonton and Vancouver Whitecaps FC. He eventually joined the FC Edmonton academy before moving to Vancouver, helping pave a pathway for Davies.

He was someone Davies looked up to. Though it's not something they ever spoke about in detail, Amanda said he and Davies also grew closer over their shared life experiences.

Amanda was born in Tanzania's Nyarugusu refugee camp to Congolese parents who fled their homeland after a civil war erupted in 1996. He was the fifth of nine children in the family. They all lived together on the refugee camp in a small home his parents built from brick. That's where he spent his formative years before immigrating to Edmonton.

Although they came from different countries, Davies and Amanda were on parallel paths that seemed destined to converge. Their experiences weren't identical, however. Davies was 5 when he landed in Canada. Amanda was 10.

While Davies felt like he grew up there, Amanda felt like he was starting an entirely new life.

"The first year you're kind of silent because you're trying to learn everything," Amanda recalled. "I remember I wanted to learn the language so badly, because I wanted to know what people were saying. I would spend hours and hours watching kids shows, like *Dora*, *Diego*, and stuff like that, just so I can learn the language."

The universal language of soccer helped ease the transition.

"Soccer became a way for me to communicate with those around me," Amanda said. "It's like, 'Hey, look, I can also play soccer, I'm not an alien.' That's where most of my friendships to this day have come from."

With Davies, Amanda saw himself as more of a big brother. Davies was also close with Amanda's younger brother, so he was always around. One year, they even spent Christmas together. Davies couldn't have asked for a better role model. Wherever he's played, Amanda has been praised for his work ethic, professionalism, and desire to succeed.

That desire, he'll tell you, stems from his upbringing.

"One hundred percent," Amanda said. "Knowing where you come from kind of fuels you to make sure you're humble, committed to what you're doing, and for me, it gives me a reason to never give up."

That's something he and Davies had in common, perhaps more than anything else.

It was never just about the goals and assists with Davies, as pretty as they were. Like Amanda, he was extremely driven, as evidenced by the countless hours they spent together in the gym after school.

He was the ultimate team player, often chasing down his teammates to celebrate their goals more than his own. And he always, *always*, had a smile on his face.

It's one of the reasons Davies was named captain at St. Nicholas in Grade 8, despite still being one of the younger players on the team.

"He made others around him better," Bossio said.

All those things were on display when Davies travelled with the Strikers to the 2015 Dallas Cup, an invite-only international youth tournament that has featured some of the best players and teams in the world. The tournament was held around Easter, which made for an "interesting trip" from Edmonton, joked Talal Al-Awaid, who was helping Huoseh coach the team. There were multiple layovers. Multiple delays. A hiccup with transportation from the airport. But they finally made it to the hotel in Dallas.

After a quick stop at Popeyes for some fried chicken and lemonade, that is.

"The kids are tired, but they're excited," Al-Awaid said. "So you have the kids that jump into the pool, you have the kids that go and set up the PlayStation right away and start getting the *FIFA* going. You start meeting all the new teams in the hotel as well . . . teams from Brazil, a team from Uruguay, and all that."

The Strikers players had freedom to roam, provided they followed a set schedule for meals, lights out, and the like. But there was one little problem.

No one could seem to find Davies.

"We were walking around the hotel, there are tons of teams, we're trying to figure out where this kid is," Al-Awaid said. "Eventually, during our hunt for Alphonso, we start going and talking to people and pointing to our crest and asking if they've seen anyone with this jacket. And some guy just points towards the gym."

There he was, drenched in sweat, doing a full workout.

"We were like, 'What are you doing? Aren't you tired?'" Al-Awaid recalled. "He's like, 'Yeah, I'm tired, but I haven't worked out today.'"

"He had it as a goal that he was going to work hard every day, train every day, and get better," Al-Awaid continued. "After this much travel, the excitement of a tournament, being in a new place you haven't been, all the kids were having fun . . . he still had the fun, he ate the Popeyes, he did all that, but he also knew that he had to work out."

Sure enough, Davies "tore that tournament apart," Al-Awaid said.

Against stiff competition, too, including academy teams affiliated with Mexican giants CF Monterrey and Pumas UNAM, as well as MLS clubs FC Dallas and Chicago Fire.

"You just had people walking around saying, 'Oh, the Canadian team is playing on Field 6. They've got this one kid. You have to go watch him,'" Al-Awaid recalled. "All of a sudden we've got 50 or 60 people watching our games, and we're just this random team from Edmonton."

For Al-Awaid, it was Davies's mindset that set him apart. There were other great athletes. There were other talented players. But what he saw from Davies as a 14-year-old in that gym?

That was rare.

"I remember going back to the room and talking to Nick and saying, 'There's something about this kid,'" he said. "'I can't pinpoint it. But with that work ethic, it's not going to matter what he decides to do in life. If he has that work ethic, he's going to succeed.'"

Those words would prove prophetic.

CHAPTER 4:
"LET ME GO"

It was a school night. But Davies had a good excuse to be staying out later than usual.

For most of the 17,863 fans in attendance at BC Place, it would have been the first time they saw him play. The crowd, including his Whitecaps academy teammates, who filled an entire row in front of the press box, roared with anticipation every time he touched the ball.

"Sweet little back heel from Davies. What were you doing when you were 15?" the official Whitecaps account tweeted in the 25th minute.

A little later, he almost brought the roof off the place.

With the ball at his feet, Davies dribbled towards the opposition defender from the left corner of the pitch. There was no one else around them. It was a true one-v-one.

As he approached the box, Davies stepped over the ball with his left foot, and then with his right, creating a little separation between him and the backpedalling defender. Without hesitation, he then took a touch towards his left, faked the cross, and cut back towards his right foot. By this point, the defender — who was nearly twice Davies's age — had lost his balance and fallen to the ground. Finally, Davies let loose a right-footed strike that split the pair of defenders protecting the goal and froze the goalkeeper only to bounce off the far post.

He didn't score, but he may as well have.

"He's a real, real exciting talent," Ottawa Fury FC head coach Paul Dalglish said after the match. "He's brilliant, for 15 years of age to do that. At 15, I couldn't even look people in the eye."

That night, as the Whitecaps defeated Ottawa 3–0 in the do-or-die second leg of the Canadian Championship semifinal, Davies became Vancouver's youngest player to start a first-team match in the 40-plus-year history of the club. And the next morning, he went to school.

He actually had a science test. Abiotic and biotic factors.

After school, as was customary, Davies showed up to train with his youth teammates at Burnaby 8 Rinks — a recreational facility that housed the academy at the time.

"Alphonso, what are you doing?" said Craig Dalrymple, the former Whitecaps academy director, who also played for the club during the Vancouver 86ers era.

"I'm ready to train, coach," he remembered Davies saying.

"You just made your debut. I'm not sure the first-team manager is going to be happy if I allow you to train with the U-16 group the day after your match. You should be in recovery."

"We don't have to tell him," Davies responded, like a 15-year-old would.

"Well, we kind of do have to tell him, because that's my job. I'll put a call in and see what they say."

The conversation went as Dalrymple suspected it would.

After all, he'd seen what transpired the night before, like everyone else. Davies was on the first-team schedule now. It was meant to be a recovery and regeneration day.

He wasn't allowed to train.

So Dalrymple explained the situation and told Davies if he wanted to stick around, he could fill up the water bottles and be the linesman for the subsequent U-16 training game, expecting him to decline the offer and trot off home.

"But no, he picked up the water bottles, filled them up, came back, grabbed the flag, and ran the line for the 11-v-11 game, as important to him to make sure he did a good job as a linesman as it was playing in his debut the day before," Dalrymple recalled. "That just speaks to his love for the sport, his passion. He just wanted to be around it, and he understood the value of being around his friends and his peers."

Remarkably, Davies's debut with the first team — defined as the most senior team in a club's structure, sitting at the very top of the pyramid — came less than a year after he joined the Whitecaps. It was a rapid ascent from Vancouver's U-16s, to the U-18s, to the second team, and eventually the first team.

And it almost never happened.

Situated along Canada's West Coast, Vancouver is the third-largest metropolitan area in the country and one of the most livable cities in the world, according to various rankings.

Guess they haven't seen the real estate prices.

The "Whitecaps" name was inspired by the natural beauty of the region. As the story goes, the club's original founder was driving across the Lions Gate Bridge when he saw the white-capped peaks of the mountains overlooking the white-capped waves beneath.

Thus, the Whitecaps were born.

Founded in 1973, the Whitecaps are one of the oldest professional soccer clubs in North America. Their claim to fame is the 1979 NASL Soccer Bowl, when they became the city's first professional sports team to win a major North American championship. The league was littered with big names. Three-time Ballon d'Or winner Johan Cruyff. Manchester United legend George Best. Famous Bayern Munich centre back Franz Beckenbauer. The great Pelé had even played a few years prior.

But the "Village of Vancouver," as an ABC commentator famously called it, emerged victorious in 1979.

The North American Soccer League folded five years later. And while Vancouver soccer supporters had more championships to celebrate in a variety of different leagues that were subsequently formed, it wasn't until 2011 that the Whitecaps officially returned to the top tier of soccer in North America: now Major League Soccer, or MLS.

Since then, success has proved elusive.

Still, as the lone MLS club in Western Canada, the Whitecaps were typically seen as the most attractive destination for the region's high-potential youth players looking to pursue a professional career. It also helped that they invested heavily in a full-time player development program, or academy, and technically had exclusive territorial rights to recruit players from Western Canada, per MLS regulations.

Dalrymple and his staff would get regular updates from the Alberta Soccer Association, based in their neighbouring province, on any progressing players to keep an eye on. Those players were usually 13, 14, or 15 years old. Then there was Davies, who was 10 or 11 when Dalrymple said he first got wind of him. The Whitecaps also had a good relationship with the St. Nicholas Soccer Academy, which had previously sent a few players to the club.

In both cases, Davies's name always came up.

"Some of the trusted people that were working in the Alberta football scene said, 'This boy is incredible,'" Dalrymple recalled.

At that point, Davies was "on the back burner," according to Dalrymple. It wasn't until he turned 13 that the Whitecaps accelerated their interest.

In the spring of 2014, Huoseh brought Davies out to Vancouver with the Strikers for a Whitecaps youth showcase. The tournament, held in nearby Surrey, was an opportunity for elite youth teams to play in front of college scouts and Whitecaps academy staff. They also got to mingle with the pros — there's a photo from that weekend in which Davies and his Strikers teammates are posing with Whitecaps first-team players Kekuta Manneh and Erik Hurtado — and attend the MLS match against LA Galaxy.

A few months later, Davies was back in Vancouver for another Whitecaps showcase. This time, it was with Alberta North. They stayed in the dorm rooms at the University of British Columbia and played against the other provincial teams from Western Canada. Davies scored a couple of goals against Saskatchewan and "dismantled" Team BC, Sergio Teixeira recalled. The best players from the tournament then participated in an all-star game on the final day.

Naturally, Davies was selected.

After the game, a Whitecaps official pulled him aside for a chat. They went over to UBC Thunderbird Stadium and sat in the bleachers. Davies didn't have a guardian there, so Teixeira tagged along and sat a few rows below them.

He also called Huoseh to keep him apprised of the situation.

"I remember using this analogy with him. It was almost like when [Cristiano] Ronaldo played with Sporting against Man United," Teixeira said. "They were like, 'These guys aren't leaving with him. We need this kid here.'"

That's when things got serious.

Over the next six months, Davies would be invited back to Vancouver for two separate trials and a third visit with his family. On the first trial, Dalrymple and his staff got the sense that Davies was too young. He was nervous. He was cautious. Emotionally, he wasn't ready for such a big move. On the second one, the Whitecaps arranged an exhibition game at Simon Fraser University, and it was clear that he'd taken a big step.

"All these parents were watching their boys for the Whitecaps," said Marco Bossio, who travelled with Davies that December. "As soon as Phonzie got the ball, the parents kind of got off their chairs and said, 'Oh boy, who is this kid?' He was just carving the field up."

Finally, on the third trip, Davies got an opportunity to train with the first team.

At that point, it was a matter of trying to get the deal over the line, according to then-Whitecaps head coach Carl Robinson.

"Probably the hardest thing was deciding what was the best thing to offer him at that time," Robinson said. "Because you had the academy, you had the [United Soccer League], and you had the first team. And without actually trying to get him from A to C quickly, or A to B quickly, the progression for all these young players needs to be measured. We didn't know how quickly he'd progress, but we thought we'd get him into the first team to see where he's at in relation to them. Then we can work backwards."

Within a couple of days, some of the senior players were lobbying for him to be signed.

For his part, Dalrymple said the moment he was truly "hooked" came during a seven-v-seven indoor game in Edmonton. He'd flown there to meet with the family and see Davies play in his own environment. What he saw was a player "doing anything he wanted to do."

Not in a selfish or disobedient way, but an "astonishing" one.

"There was a free kick for his team on the halfway line," Dalrymple recalled. "It was probably 30 yards from the goal. I'm just like, 'He's going to shoot this thing.' There were probably 8 to 10 players between him and the goal. And he just smashed this thing past everyone. It went past the keeper, the keeper didn't even move. I mean, jeez, who does that? Who even thinks to do that in an indoor game?"

"Craig's jaw just dropped," said Huoseh, who also arranged to have his Strikers team play a couple of friendly matches with the Whitecaps for additional viewings of Davies.

"My grandmother would have picked him out," Dalrymple said. "He was just *that* good."

There was no denying his talent. It was more of a question as to whether all parties involved felt Davies was ready to leave his comfort zone, his support system, and essentially start a new life in a new city. To that point, he'd never even had a job — an application to McDonald's went unanswered. This wasn't just a matter of changing soccer teams.

"It was important that all the key people in his life were ready and supportive of it . . . and he also needed to be ready," Dalrymple said. "Our approach was putting zero pressure on him. It had to be his choice when he came, if he came. All we could do is say, 'This is what we're here to offer you, this is the environment, this is how we think it's going to help you, you need to be ready to come into this.'"

Davies felt he was ready. But his parents had their concerns.

They didn't know anything about Vancouver. They couldn't just hand their son over to a bunch of strangers and jeopardize the life they worked so hard for him to have.

So they refused.

"When we came here, nobody ever came to the house and said Alphonso is on drugs, smoking, nothing. Nobody, never, ever. So who will look after him?" Debeah wondered.

"At that time, he was 14," Victoria added. "I was afraid. I'd seen some kids, sometimes I see them on TV, or I see them on the street, what they're doing. I don't want him to become a bad boy. So I told him . . . he's not leaving until he's maybe 16 or 17."

Initially, Victoria held firm. But as the conversations continued, she warmed to the idea.

The Whitecaps explained that Davies, like all their academy players who came from out of town, would live with a host or billet family responsible for his well-being.

He would also be required to not only attend his classes but apply himself in school and stay out of trouble to even step onto a soccer pitch. The Whitecaps had a partnership with Burnaby Central Secondary School, just down the street from the academy training facility, which housed all their student athletes as part of a holistic development program.

"We said, 'OK, make sure that Alphonso goes to school every day,'" Debeah recalled. "*Every* day."

They were assured that would be the case.

In addition to letter grades, students in British Columbia are evaluated on a work habit scale — excellent, good, satisfactory, and needs improvement. The Whitecaps expected all their academy players to receive an excellent or good evaluation to remain a part of the team.

"That simply means they're attending, they're working hard, they're handing things in on time, the type of stuff you'd expect out of a student who needs to be focused," said longtime Whitecaps academy staffer Dave Irvine, who met with the Davies family in Edmonton to discuss the schooling structure. "It was clearly very important to them. We never really discussed grades, but they wanted him to graduate, they wanted to make sure that he was attending everything and had support if he needed it."

It also helped that Vancouver was only a 90-minute flight from Edmonton. Davies could easily go back home during breaks. In-person visits could be arranged quickly.

They certainly were during the recruitment process.

On one of his final trips to Edmonton, Dalrymple brought some Whitecaps apparel along with him for Davies. A jersey, tracksuit, hat, and scarf. Nothing out of the ordinary.

"I've got a bag in my rental car that I want to give to Alphonso," Dalrymple told Victoria.

She asked what was in it.

"I said, 'It's just some Whitecaps swag,'" he recalled. "She says, 'No, he doesn't get that, he doesn't get that until he's earned it, until he deserves it.'"

The Whitecaps weren't the only team knocking on the door.

The city of Edmonton had its own professional team, FC Edmonton, competing in the second tier of the North American soccer pyramid, a rung below MLS. Jeff Paulus, the longtime technical director of FC Edmonton's academy, often conducted guest coaching sessions with some of the youth teams in the city, including the Strikers.

And that's how he was first introduced to Davies.

"There were a couple of boys on that team, Alphonso Davies and Oscar Miranda, who I really liked working with," Paulus said. "They both really stood out as different players. So I offered them both spots in our academy."

Miranda accepted, but it was decided that Davies would stay with the Strikers.

Later on, as Vancouver's interest intensified, he did spend a couple of months training with the FC Edmonton academy to help prepare for the next level. Paulus said he'd been talking to Dalrymple "quite a bit" and knew Davies was likely headed there.

So they offered to give him extra training.

"He was never in the FC Edmonton academy," Paulus said. "We just provided a training ground for him for a few months."

During that time, Paulus's group played a couple of games against a high-level training squad from Calgary. As usual, Davies was younger than the other players. And yet "there wasn't a player around doing the things that he would do," Paulus said.

At that point, Paulus said FC Edmonton made a final pitch to sign him upon recommendation from their head coach at the time, Colin Miller.

"When Colin saw him play, he said, 'No no, we can't lose this kid,'" Paulus recalled. "So we then, of course, put an offer in to try and keep him here with us. And he made the right choice. Quite honestly, he made the right choice and he chose Vancouver. I was doing my job for the club that employed me to offer him to stay with us, but deep down inside I knew it wasn't the right thing to do for the kid.

"For me, he was going to the right environment," Paulus added. "He was going to an MLS academy. It was where he needed to go. I thought he would have outgrown FC Edmonton very quickly. I don't know we would have been able to offer him what the Whitecaps could have."

Finally, it was agreed that Davies would finish Grade 9 in Edmonton before moving to Vancouver in August 2015, a few months before his 15th birthday. The Whitecaps' pitch paid off.

But it was a promise from Davies that sealed the deal.

"I'm going to be the same," Victoria remembered him saying. "I will not go to Vancouver and change. I will make you guys proud.

"Let me go."

CHAPTER 5:
NUMBER 67

"**Y**ou suck."

Davies had just joined the Whitecaps academy. It was a step up from anything he'd experienced before. Everyone was a bit better. Everything was a bit faster. He was messing up more than he usually did.

And as he recounted to FC Bayern.tv, one of his new teammates let him know it.

"You're not going to make it," they added.

If you ask Davies about that initial period in Vancouver, he'll tell you he was a "nervous wreck," as he wrote in *The Players' Tribune*. He'll tell you it was a real struggle. But if you ask almost anyone else, maybe aside from that one teammate, they'll tell you it was unlike anything they'd ever seen.

Theo Bair, who joined the Whitecaps academy that same year, remembers the first time he saw Davies play. It was an intrasquad game. The first half was dull. Nothing really happened.

Then in the second half, Davies took over, scoring three goals in the first 10 minutes.

"Right after the game, on the way home, I called my dad," Bair recalled. "My dad asked how the intrasquad went. I said, 'Dad, I think I just played with the best player I have ever played with in my life.'"

Davies played less than 20 official matches for the Whitecaps youth academy teams before signing a professional contract, but he certainly made his mark. In his first five league games with the U-16s, he scored five goals and racked up a boatload of assists to boot. That included a hat-trick against the San Diego Surf on a sweltering hot September afternoon at the Scripps Ranch High School.

They were his first official goals with the club. And they were very different ones.

First, he got behind the back line and slipped one past the goal-keeper with his left foot. Then he powered home a header from close range. And finally, he completed the hat-trick with a right-footed half volley from the top of the box. One goal with his left foot, one with his head, one with his right foot.

This wasn't a one-trick pony.

The Whitecaps U-16s won four of those first five matches and tied the other. Davies's coaches remember him scoring or assisting every single one of the team's goals during that initial stretch.

"It was just ball to his feet, he would touch it around someone, and then boom, he's gone down the line," Bair said. "No one could keep up with him."

After a few months with the U-16s, it was clear Davies needed to be moved up an age group. So it was on to the U-18s. In his very first appearance with them, he scored two minutes after subbing on.

How's that for a first impression?

Davies had just turned 15 years old. He was now playing against 16-, 17-, and even 18-year-olds.

"And making it look easy," said Whitecaps academy coach Rich Fagan, who oversaw the U-18s at the time. "It was like, well, I can't really give him instruction from the sideline. Because when he loses the ball, he just goes and wins it. And then when he wins it, he's in on goal pretty much every time. That's when I realized, 'Holy shit, we have something here.' Like, this is special."

It wasn't just what Davies was doing on the field, either. Rather, his coaches saw someone that oozed character. He wasn't cocky. He wasn't self-centred.

He was a leader.

"You never had to ask him to pick up a cone, clean up the bibs, or do his chores around the facility," Fagan said. "He was proactive in that sense. In fact, he would be the type of kid where if he's recognized that somebody hasn't maybe done what they should be doing, he'll probably do it for them."

It always just seemed like Davies could read a room. When he first travelled to Vancouver with his parents and younger siblings, for example, Craig Dalrymple said that Davies was almost "mothering" in the way he made sure they had everything they needed.

Then there was the time Dalrymple had Davies over for dinner in those early academy days. Dalrymple has three daughters, all younger than Davies. But he found a way to relate to each of them. He was dancing in the living room, playing Lego — little things that went a long way in forming a connection.

"He has this tremendous awareness of individuals around him," Dalrymple said. "Even in a changing room with his peers on his team, he's not got the blinders on and unaware of the other stresses and emotions going on in the locker room. He's generally tapped into all that stuff."

It's part of the reason why Davies managed to quickly adapt and integrate into every new situation he was thrown into. That would be a key theme of his time with the Whitecaps and throughout his career.

It was certainly the case when he first got a look with the big boys.

At the time, the Whitecaps had a pair of *really* big boys on their first-team roster. There was Kendall Waston, who was 6-foot-5 and 215 pounds. And there was his 6-foot-1, 175-pound centre back partner, Pa-Modou Kah. They were physical. They were intimidating. And whenever a young player started to train with the first team, they liked to make their presence known.

Or better yet felt.

"When you come in, we're going to rough you up a little bit," Kah said. "Just a little bit of a welcome, a little bit of an old-school method, to test those young kids."

So when Davies got invited to train with the first team, they knew what to do.

"I remember Kendall roughing him up first. I roughed him again, then the third time he kind of snuck away from Kendall," Kah recalled. "That kind of caught the eyes of the rest of the players.

"And you're like, 'OK, there's something there.'"

On January 30, 2016, the Whitecaps released the names of the 38 players who would be travelling with the first team for their preseason training camp in Tucson, Arizona.

Near the bottom of the list, there was a surprise invitee from the academy.

Forward.

Number 67.

Alphonso Davies.

It's not often a 15-year-old comes anywhere close to an MLS training camp. And Davies hadn't even been a part of the academy for six months at that point.

But there he was.

And there he was the next day, with a GoPro strapped to his head, running back and forth as the Whitecaps and other passengers waited to board their flight at the Vancouver International Airport.

"Faster, faster!" Kah yelled. "That's too slow!"

Once they finally got on the flight, Kah pulled some strings to get Davies a flight attendant's scarf and have him walk down the aisle serving drinks, along with a fellow Whitecaps rookie. Davies, the youngest player in camp, was unfazed by his initiation.

It was a sign of things to come.

Thanks to his strong showing in the preseason and dominant performances with the academy, Davies moved on from the youth ranks and signed his first professional contract just three weeks later. Now, for the first time in his life, he was making some money. A joint bank account with his mom was promptly set up at BMO, and he was off and running. Initially, he joined the Whitecaps' second team in the United Soccer League, which is a tier lower than MLS but still a professional league made up of adults and other top prospects.

He played his first professional game in April and scored his first goal in May.

"He was just this young teenager that was head and shoulders better than everyone else," said longtime Whitecaps midfielder Russell Teibert, who was in the stands that afternoon at UBC Thunderbird Stadium. "I remember him doing a backflip after he scored. I was already kind of in awe of this kid then."

He wasn't the only one.

By July, Carl Robinson and his assistants had already seen enough to offer him an MLS deal.

"If you're good enough, you're old enough," Robinson would often say.

Seated at a round table in the office of the club president, Davies carefully reviewed the contract, initialled the bottom corner of each page, and signed on the dotted line.

At 15 years and 256 days old, he became the youngest active player in MLS.

The Whitecaps had a match the very next day against Orlando. Davies wasn't expecting to get his MLS debut so soon, but Robinson called his name on the sideline with 13 minutes remaining.

He was going in.

"I froze. I think I actually asked him, 'Really?'" Davies wrote in *The Players' Tribune*.

Just months earlier, Davies was playing on high school soccer fields with only a few friends and family in attendance. Now, he was about to step onto the pitch in front of 22,120 rabid fans at BC Place, one of Canada's largest sport venues, which had previously hosted the Winter Olympic Games as well as the FIFA Women's World Cup Final.

"I was *sooo* nervous," Davies continued in *The Players' Tribune*. "And the problem when you're nervous is that you don't really want to touch the ball. You don't want anyone to pass to you. You don't want to make a mistake. But then a long ball came toward me and a defender came chasing after me. I was like, *He's gonna hit me. I'm gonna get rocked.* Yet somehow I brought the ball down, took a touch inside and fired off a shot. Even though it didn't go in, right then and there I got confidence.

"After that, things happened quickly."

They sure did.

Within his first couple of years as a professional, Davies would become the youngest goalscorer in the history of the Whitecaps, United Soccer League, Canadian Championship, Canadian men's national team, Concacaf Champions League, and Concacaf Gold Cup.

The goals and assists didn't come as easy in MLS, but it seemed like Davies would create at least one moment of magic every match he played — usually by embarrassing an opposition defender, or several.

Remember, he was still a teenager. He couldn't even win the club's man of the match award because it was sponsored by Budweiser. Only players of legal drinking age — 19 in Vancouver — were eligible. He won the award just once during his three years in MLS, and that was due to an oversight from club staff.

It was October 2, 2016.

The Whitecaps were hosting Seattle Sounders FC, their biggest rival.

Davies was electric from start to finish. The highlight? A run down the right wing in which he rounded a defender along the endline while remarkably keeping the ball in play, before eventually getting yanked down to earn the Whitecaps a penalty kick.

As it so happened, there was a scout from famed English Premier League club Manchester United FC in the building that evening specifically to watch Davies play. Word got out in the local newspaper, *The Province*. The official MLS website reported on it too. And that's when interest in the "teenage prodigy," as media around the world started to call him, really began to pick up steam.

But the Whitecaps tried their best to shelter him.

Many years prior, a young American named Freddy Adu broke into MLS at age 14 with D.C. United. He was the only player younger than Davies to have played in the league. He was anointed the saviour of American soccer. They called him the next Pelé. The hype machine was in full force. And ultimately, it contributed to his downfall.

No one wanted to see Davies go down that same path.

Robinson was keenly aware of Adu's story — their playing careers in MLS briefly overlapped. He'd also seen and admired how some of his friends and former teammates, such as Robbie Keane and

Aaron Ramsey, had been brought along and "protected" by their respective clubs as highly touted teenagers before becoming English Premier League stars.

So he tried to draw from their experiences.

Interview requests were seldom granted in Davies's early years. And there were a lot of them. It was almost a daily occurrence, in fact. The Whitecaps would make Davies available to media around major milestones and for certain feature pieces, but he was spared from the daily grind of fielding questions after every training session and game.

They figured Davies was going to be doing media for the rest of his life. At 15 years old, they didn't want to throw him into the deep end right away.

"I understand why people wanted to dig deep into Alphonso's background, what he was like, where his head was, get to know him, but my whole thought process was, you have plenty of time to get to know him," Robinson said. "Let his football do the talking. He doesn't need to be on every back page of a paper or every front of a magazine, on every talk show, on every *SportsCentre*, like Freddy Adu was."

Ironically, the day Davies made his first-team debut against Ottawa, he was featured on the back page of *The Province* newspaper in Vancouver. However, it came with the very message the Whitecaps were trying to promote.

The headline? "HOLD THE HYPE."

"Talented 15-year-old Alphonso Davies makes his Whitecaps first-team debut today in Ottawa, but let's not gush too much about the kid — we don't want to ruin him," the subheadline read.

Robinson said there were "some battles" with the club's media relations staff. And there were times when he was "overruled." But he admitted those were few and far between.

"I'll be fair to the club," he said. "They were very good in relation to that."

On the pitch, Davies was used sporadically. He would come on as a substitute most matches but would rarely start. In fact, he started only 11 of his first 34 appearances in MLS. And those came over one and a half seasons.

Many were left wanting more.

But internally, there were concerns about consistency, burnout, and potential injuries as his body developed. The Whitecaps sports science staff would monitor all the players' training loads, heart rates, max velocities, and other metrics. And they found that Davies didn't have a middle gear.

Every game, every training session, it was full steam ahead.

"Even though he was such a young player, the metrics he was reaching already were so high," Robinson said. "We actually had to put a curb on him. We had to bring him down a level or two."

These are some of the considerations that went into deciding whether to start Davies and when he might need a game off. Usually, they had a set plan in place.

Sometimes, plans change.

It was the beginning of Davies's second season and he was off to a hot start. He'd just started Vancouver's first four games, including the Concacaf Champions League semifinal against Mexican power-house Tigres UANL. More than 30,000 hostile Tigres fans filled their stadium, just north of Monterrey. It had been billed as one of the biggest games in Whitecaps history. And Davies, now 16, was one of the best players on the field.

Four days later, the Whitecaps had a game against Toronto FC back in Vancouver. After emptying the tank in Mexico, Davies wasn't scheduled to start. But Robinson said he was "guided" to reconsider because the game was being broadcast on Sky Sports in England. Davies was already on the radar of some high-profile European clubs. This would be an opportunity for them, and others, to see what he could do.

Robinson said he wasn't forced into anything. Ultimately, it was his decision.

"I ended up playing him. And he was awful."

So Robinson subbed Davies out of the game at halftime, which he almost never did with anyone, and apologized for putting him into that position. One media member called it "Davies's worst game of the season." Another referred to his performance as "anonymous."

"You get things right and you get things wrong," Robinson said. "I'm not here to say I got everything right, because I didn't. That was one example where I got it badly wrong."

There's a phrase Liverpool uses with its young players, as inspired by the late and legendary head coach Bob Paisley. Their assistant manager, Pep Lijnders, shared it in his training camp diary published on the team's official website in 2021. It goes: "We search for a player who nutmegs Virgil van Dijk in training but steps politely aside for him in the corridor."

That was Davies.

Around the first team, he was quiet at first. He stayed in his lane. He didn't ruffle any feathers. Some of the older players on the team, like Kah, helped show him the way.

Mainly, Kah wanted Davies to know that he was there for him. But he also tried to help prepare him for what was coming. Not only as a professional soccer player.

As a professional soccer player who is Black.

"If you're a Black athlete, wherever you are, if you're doing well, you're one of us," Kah said. "But the moment you're not doing well, people refer to your name or your real background. It's not going to be the Canadian Alphonso Davies. It's going to be the refugee Alphonso Davies. Anybody can say, 'No, we're not thinking like that, but that's the reality. [I wanted to] make sure he understood the pitfalls that could come with that. The fame and everything, that's one side of the game. But there's also the side of the game that can spit you out quickly as well, and all you gotta do is just one little thing that people don't like."

As the first-ever Black man to represent the Norwegian national team, Kah spoke from experience. People might hold you to higher standards, he explained. People might look at you differently. These are some of the lessons he tried to instill in Davies.

Albeit rare, there were a few teachable moments along the way. One time, Davies showed up to the training facility wearing sandals, which resulted in a scolding.

"Nobody is going to the beach," Kah told him.

Robinson also had conversations with Davies about his habits the night before a game, such as playing video games until one or two o'clock in the morning, or walking along the beach eating ice cream late at night.

Whenever these topics came up, Davies would usually nod his head and smile.

"He was very forthcoming," Robinson said. "He never lied to me once. He was open, he was honest. And you just knew straight away, when you actually got to know him more, that he was going to go a long, long way in football. His head was screwed on, he understood what he wanted, he was totally focused. If he made a mistake, he didn't make it again.

"Or I didn't find out again."

Davies was always taught to respect his elders. He wouldn't dare talk back. So whenever he was around his coaches or older teammates, he tried his best to remain respectful.

"They're grown men, they have kids, they're worried about bills and stuff like that," he said in 2017. "As kids, we don't worry about that. We just go around having fun."

In a way, Davies was living two different lives in Vancouver.

Around his peers, he was a self-proclaimed "15-year-old goof." The life of the party. A true extrovert. He and his friends would go to the mall to eat and play games like *Just Dance*, in which they mimicked the dance moves shown on the screen. Or they'd hang out at someone's house and play video games.

Sometimes they'd even talk to girls.

"I do talk to them, sometimes, not really," Davies joked in 2016.

At school, he had a particular affinity for Culinary Arts, in which the students prepared large portions of food that would be served in the cafeteria at lunchtime. In the kitchen, he wasn't 15-year-old professional soccer player Alphonso Davies.

He was "Chef D."

"In the beginning, he was definitely shy and a little more reserved. By the end, he was preparing food while singing and dancing," said his Culinary Arts teacher, Heather Parkes. "He would sit there and belt out songs while he was chopping up chicken or dicing vegetables."

One week, Davies might be responsible for preparing the main course. The next week, he might be at the sandwich station or in the bakery making cookies. Parkes said one of the reasons Davies got put into the class was to give him the life skill of being able to cook, since he was away from family. He knew how to do some things, he told her, but he wasn't confident.

"He said he made what he could when he was watching his siblings," Parkes recalled.

His "dream meal," according to Parkes, was a nice pasta dinner with garlic bread and Caesar salad to cook for his girlfriend at the time, Jordyn Huitema.

"He wanted to make something more traditionally Canadian," Parkes said. "At his billet family, that may be something they would have. But that wasn't how [his own family] ate at home."

Over time, the kitchen became Davies's home base at school. His safe space.

The one place he could unapologetically be himself.

"If he wasn't having a good day, somehow he always ended up in there, sitting in my office," Parkes said. "I got to know him well enough that I could tell when something was off on him. Like when he's not in a good mood, he gets really quiet. So I'd be able to pick up on that. 'OK, what's wrong?' 'Oh, I didn't have a good practice.' Or, you know, 'I'm just missing home.' In the beginning, he missed being at home a lot."

That was something Robinson became aware of as well. He'd never hear it from Davies directly, but from some of the senior players who were close to him. So every now and again, he'd give him a few days off to fly back to Edmonton.

"When I asked him, he would say he's fine," Robinson recalled. "He wouldn't want to tell me because he wanted to train every day and play every minute of every game, so he would never tell me. But the players would. So I'd make it non-negotiable. I'd say, 'Phonzie, I want you to go home.' And as soon as I gave him the avenue to go home, he would."

Davies was in a completely different world than the rest of his teammates.

He lived in Burnaby with his billet parents, not far from his high school and the Whitecaps academy home base. But it was a 90-minute trek via public transit to the University of British Columbia, the westernmost point of the city, where the Whitecaps' first team trained.

And he wasn't old enough to drive alone at first. So there were times he took the SkyTrain to meet up with David Edgar, a veteran player who joined the Whitecaps around the same time that Davies broke into the first team, and Edgar drove him the rest of the way.

"I said, 'Listen, if you meet me at my house every morning at 7:30, I will drive you to training. You'll be early, you'll be one of the first ones in there. It'll be good. It means you don't have to transit all the way and whatnot,'" Edgar recalled. "And he did. I said to him, though, 'If you're late, I will leave.'"

That only happened once.

There was also the time that Edgar was running a bit late himself. As he was getting ready, his wife got a text message from her cousin, who was living with them at the time.

"We have someone on the porch playing with Lila," the text read, referencing Edgar's four-year-old daughter.

Guess who?

"I was like, 'Oh, don't worry, it's Alphonso,'" Edgar laughed. "He just came in, my daughter was downstairs, she had just gotten out of bed, and they were playing. It was like a wounded bird at the back patio that he was helping fly away."

Davies had his learner's licence at the time, meaning he was allowed to drive with a supervisor. So on the way home after training, depending on how they were both feeling, Edgar would toss Davies the keys and let him take the wheel.

"I didn't know if he'd be messing around or anything, but it was laser focus," Edgar said.

It was actually Parkes's husband who taught Davies how to drive. On gamedays, he'd pick Davies up at his billet home in Burnaby and let him drive to BC Place, down Hastings Street.

"He got to pull into the parking lot and park so that he got to feel like he was one of the players, like the rest of them," Parkes said. "I think there was one time somebody was taking pictures and he parked really bad and then he had to back up and park again. I'm like, that's the reality of learning how to drive, kiddo. It's not going to be perfect every time!"

Davies was a quick learner — behind the wheel, on the field, and even in the classroom. He struggled with classes like English and math, but he tried his best to keep up.

Denise Davis, who was the vice-president at Burnaby Central Secondary School, remembers seeing his first assignment in Grade 10 English. It was just a couple of sentences. A few months later, the English teacher remarked how impressed she was with his improvement.

"His goal and intention was always to do well academically," Davis said. "It just wasn't that meaningful and important to him. But it was to his parents. He just had so much love, respect, and appreciation for them that there was no way he'd let them down."

As Davies became more of a regular on the first team, he eventually had to switch to online classes to accommodate the more demanding schedule. The club also had a private tutor come to the training facility to help him with his homework. He didn't really have to be at the school anymore.

But that didn't stop him.

Anytime he'd have a day off from training, he'd be back in the school kitchen with Parkes. Or he'd be on the basketball court, shooting hoops with Bair and some of their friends.

"He just wanted to be a teenager," Parkes said. "I think the school was that place for him."

There were times when Davies had to be chased down to complete his assignments. Or when he'd need some extra help. But the teachers and school administrators were always there for him. Both Parkes and Davis spent their own time tutoring him. They didn't have to do that.

They wanted to.

"All the teachers loved him," said Dave Irvine, the Whitecaps academy staffer who would get regular reports from the school. "It all came back to, he just has this aura about him. Happy, big smile, welcoming, and warm to absolutely everybody."

Davies genuinely appreciated the support.

On March 31, 2017, Davis retired from her post as Burnaby Central vice-president. At that point, Davies wasn't attending the school regularly anymore. But that Friday, he showed up and surprised Davis with an autographed jersey as a retirement gift.

"Thank you for everything," she remembered him saying.

Davis assumed that Irvine or Parkes helped arrange the visit. So she reached out to each of them individually and thanked them. But neither of them knew anything about it.

It was all Davies.

"I thought that was just so thoughtful and caring," Davis said. "And really indicative of the whole person that he is. He had a big heart. He had the biggest heart in the entire world."

Davis always had a soft spot for Davies. From the very first meeting they had, she was struck by his firm handshake, solid eye contact, and big smile. He was well-mannered. He was humble. And that never, ever changed.

"We were worried, once he got signed to the Whitecaps at that age, like oh my gosh, the minute he'd start earning some money and stuff, how's this going to change him?" Davis recalled. "But it didn't. It really didn't at all. It was who he was."

Since Davies was so young, and his parents weren't around, Davis tried her best to look out for him. At one point, she noticed that "a few young gals" had been bringing him a latte from Starbucks every morning. So she called him into her office to talk about it.

"Do you understand what is really happening here?" she asked.

"Oh yes, Mrs. Davis, I get it," she remembered him saying. "They think if they buy me a latte, then I'll be interested in them or whatever."

"Everyone has different goals, focuses, and aspirations in life. These girls are lovely, but their aspirations and goals are completely different than yours. So you need to keep that in mind."

"No no, I got this, I got this."

He didn't fall for it. But he did ask her if he could still accept the lattes.

Davies never lost sight of his goals. As he told Davis in their first meeting, he wanted to become a professional soccer player. That was his focus.

He wasn't going to let anything get in the way.

"We had some interesting characters in that program that we had to terminate from a school perspective," Davis said. "I was really worried they were going to draw Alphonso in. But he was grounded, spiritually, morally, and he could see through people. He could see what their true intentions were. That never blurred for him. And I believe that grounding and that foundation, which came from his parents and upbringing, is what raised him to the level where he is today."

CHAPTER 6:
"MY NAME IS
ALPHONSO DAVIES"

"Good afternoon. Bonjour."
Standing on a spotlighted stage at Moscow's Expocentre, Davies began his address.

In front of him, Davies saw an enormous auditorium jam-packed with some of the most influential people in soccer. There were rows upon rows of international dignitaries seated at the fixed white tables spanning the width of the hall. Legends of the game. Media from all around the world.

On either side of the auditorium hung the national flags of FIFA's 200-plus member associations. Combined with the green of the turf-lined stage, and the vibrance of the big screen behind it, they added a splash of colour to an otherwise dimly lit space.

It was Davies, though, that shone brightest.

He wore a red Canada track jacket, black pants, and white Air Jordan sneakers, standing out amongst the sea of black and navy suits in the crowd.

Right next to Davies, on a smaller podium, sat the crown jewel of the sport.

The FIFA World Cup.

It was the eve of the 2018 tournament. The opening match between hosts Russia and Saudi Arabia would take place just 10 minutes down the road at Moscow's 81,000-seat Luzhniki Stadium.

But first, there was some business to take care of.

Every year, FIFA Congress meets to determine the best way forward for the sport. It's defined as the "supreme legislative body of global football," or in other words, "the United Nations of Football." From Afghanistan to Zimbabwe, a total of 211 national soccer associations have a seat at the table.

The 68th FIFA Congress was held on June 13, 2018.

It was a five-hour program comprised of 15 agenda items. They reviewed financial statements, voted on budgets and changes to statutes, and discussed various proposals. Russian president Vladimir Putin even made an address, as did FIFA president Gianni Infantino.

But those were all appetizers for the main course.

Item 13 on the agenda was a vote to determine the host for the 2026 FIFA World Cup. There were two bids on the ballot: one from Morocco, and a joint North American bid from Canada, Mexico, and the United States — named "United 2026." Each bid had 15 minutes to present before the vote.

The world was watching. FIFA had a live stream running throughout, and many TV networks jumped in at this point of the proceeding.

United 2026 was up first.

Davies led the six-person delegation onto the stage. He was joined by fellow up-and-coming athletes from Mexico and the United States, as well as the presidents of the three respective soccer associations.

Their entrance was orderly. They walked in single file.

You could hear a pin drop as Davies approached the podium, which had been set on the edge of the stage within a painted white circle to replicate the centre of a soccer pitch. He stepped onto the platform, placed his speech down, briefly looked to his left, where Infantino and other members of FIFA Council were seated, and began speaking.

"Good afternoon. Bonjour," he commenced.

"It's a great honour to speak to you today. My name is Alphonso Davies. My parents are from Liberia and fled the civil war. I was born in Ghana in a refugee camp. It was a hard life. But when I was five years old, a country called Canada welcomed us in. And the boys on the football team made me feel at home."

Then the clip that would be shared endlessly back home for years to come.

"Today," he said emphatically, "I'm 17 years old. And I'm playing for the men's national team. And I'm a *proud* Canadian citizen."

In that moment, Davies flashed his brimming smile, made even more endearing by the braces that shone on his teeth. It was a smile that could have lit up a nation, let alone this auditorium.

Now it was time to bring it home.

"My dream is to someday compete in the World Cup. Maybe even in my hometown of Edmonton," he continued. "I've played matches in Canada, Mexico, and the United States. The people of North America have *always* welcomed me. If given the opportunity, I know they'll welcome you."

With one more smile for good measure, Davies ended with a simple "Thank you."

In those 55 seconds, Davies introduced himself to the world. Some already knew what he was about as a player. Some had heard his story.

But now everyone knew *him*.

"That day, on that podium, when he spoke, people saw a real person," said Canadian men's national team head coach John Herdman, who was watching from afar in Toronto, where a press conference was planned in anticipation of a favourable result. "That moment was a young 17-year-old refugee speaking from the heart. He touched the heart of not only the people in this country, but probably every representative from around the world. And not many people can do that in a moment like that."

Sprinkled between a couple of video presentations, the five remaining members of United 2026's contingent also had a chance to speak. Morocco got its 15 minutes as well.

Finally, four and a half hours into the agenda, it was time for the vote.

Using an electronic voting system, each of the eligible member associations present had 15 seconds to make their selection. Within a minute, the results were in.

One hundred and three votes for United 2026. Sixty-five votes for Morocco.

For the first time ever, three nations would co-host a World Cup. For the first time ever, men's World Cup matches would be played in Canada.

They'd done it.

And Davies was front and centre.

"It's a moment that hopefully will change the landscape in our sport," Herdman said. "You can't look past the amount of work that was done to bring Canada to this World Cup by the many people who travelled the countries and did what they had to do, but I think when Alphonso spoke, it just became a done deal. It was inevitable."

Terence Szuplat knows a good speaker when he sees one.

He spent nearly eight years as a speechwriter for Barack Obama and accompanied the president on visits to more than 40 countries. Aside from a couple of months at the start, he worked at the White House for the duration of Obama's administration.

Szuplat specializes in helping people and organizations tell their story to the world. It's what he tried to do with Obama. And it's what he tried to do with the United 2026 bid.

"We quickly realized that even though it was going to be a global campaign where the three federations would have to travel around the world and make their case, the big moment would be the presentation in Moscow," said Szuplat, who had already been working with U.S. Soccer before getting involved with the World Cup bid. "All that campaign came down to 15 minutes."

Rather than simply having the head of federations speak, it was decided that involving three young players — one from each country — would be more impactful.

So each of the federations was asked to nominate some players.

Canada Soccer put forward four names.

71

"But they made it very clear who their preference was," Szuplat said.

Szuplat hadn't heard of Davies at that point. But after reviewing some of the materials Canada Soccer sent, he quickly realized "that it had to be Alphonso."

The overarching theme for North America's bid was "Football for All," the ability for this World Cup to unify and transcend borders and cultures, which made Davies the perfect spokesperson. It was a bit ironic, however, considering the political climate in the U.S.

Donald Trump's presidency had some wondering whether it was the right time for the U.S. to host a World Cup. The country's foreign policies, including travel bans against several Muslim-majority countries, had been heavily criticized. Its international reputation had taken a big hit. For that reason, Szuplat said the U.S. felt like the bid's "weak link," in a sense.

"As our bid leaders travelled the world and heard this, we were increasingly concerned that global animosity towards Trump might cost votes and undermine the bid," Szuplat said. "Even though Alphonso had already been chosen, we realized that one of the most effective ways to push back on the things that people around the world maybe didn't like about the United States at that moment was to remind them about the things they do like about the United States and North America. And that's our history of welcoming immigrants and refugees, our diversity, our hospitality to people around the world. And that was exactly what Alphonso embodied. He embodied that spirit in the story of his life."

The opportunity to speak at FIFA Congress was presented to Davies just over a month before the event. At first, he was a bit hesitant.

The Whitecaps had a short break from their season for the start of the 2018 FIFA World Cup, and Davies initially planned on using it to visit family back home in Edmonton.

Those working on the bid also had some concerns due to Davies's availability. He was busy with the Whitecaps. It was hard to get in touch with him.

Days went by before they got a commitment.

"When they explained what was going to happen, I got excited," Davies told reporters upon his return from Russia. "It's a great privilege and I'm glad that they picked me to share my story."

Crafting his story into one minute was very much a collaborative effort.

One of the biggest misconceptions about speechwriters, Szuplat said, is that they put words in someone else's mouth. That couldn't be further from the truth. Rather, Szuplat drew on Davies's previous interviews and spoke with him on the phone to flush out his story.

This was Davies's story. These were Davies's words.

"I think I wrote something about his daily life in the refugee camp, which he told me was not true," Szuplat recalled. "I had misunderstood something I had read. So he was very intent on making sure it was accurate and true, which was very encouraging."

Even then, Szuplat said he and the others were "holding their breath" that Davies would make it to Moscow. In the days leading up to FIFA Congress, a mandatory rehearsal was held in London, England. It was made clear that all the speakers had to be there. And they all were.

Except Davies.

He was Vancouver's most important player at that point. He had games. He had training. He couldn't just up and leave.

Right until the very end, there were backups lined up for each speaker. The feeling was, if anyone was going to have to pull out, it was probably going to be Davies.

"We would get these updates. Is he on the way to the airport? Is he on the plane? Is the plane taking off?" Szuplat recalled. "This was like a military operation, you know, to get Alphonso Davies to Moscow. Has the plane landed? Who's picking him up? Is he en route? The car brought him to the hotel in Moscow where we were practising, he finally entered the room, and everyone just let out a sigh of relief because he was finally there."

There was no time to waste.

Szuplat had been working with the other speakers for days. But this was going to be the first time he heard Davies recite his speech. He wasn't quite sure what to expect.

So they got to practising right away.

"He blew us away," Szuplat said. "He blew me away. When he smiles, his face lights up, the whole room lights up, everybody around him lights up. He just has a gift."

Davies knew this was a big deal.

But the magnitude of what was about to happen didn't quite sink in until the day before the event, when they were able to rehearse their speeches at the venue.

"When I walked into the place, I was shocked," Davies said. "I didn't think it was going to be that big."

He had never spoken to that large a crowd. Not even close. In fact, just a year prior, he said that public speaking was the one thing about himself that he wanted to improve upon the most.

All the speakers were given some tips to stay grounded up on stage. Pick a few people seated in different parts of the audience and pretend like you're speaking to them directly, they were told. They were even taught how to say "good afternoon" in the right tone.

But with Davies, there was very little coaching needed.

"One of the things that always stuck with me is when he said, 'It's my great honour to speak to you today,' and he put his hand over his heart," Szuplat said. "I don't think we coached him to do that. I think that was just truly from his heart. And when he said, 'Today, I'm a proud Canadian citizen,' and the smile lit up his face, I mean, you can't coach that. You can't teach that. That came from him and that came from his heart. It just shows why he was the right person for that moment."

Szuplat said helping bring the World Cup to North America was "one of the coolest things" he's ever been a part of and one of his proudest accomplishments as a professional. And keep in mind, this is someone who worked in the White House for close to a decade.

It helped that his son was a big soccer fan.

"So here I was, I'd written speeches for the president of the United States for nearly eight years," Szuplat said. "But when I told my son that I was getting to work with Alphonso Davies, he was more impressed with that than my White House experience. He couldn't believe it."

So when it was all said and done, Szuplat asked Davies to record a short video message for his son. It's something they both treasure to this day.

"He gave that to us," Szuplat said. "I'm always going to be grateful for him."

Everyone who was in Moscow as part of the United 2026 bid developed a special bond.

It was certainly the case with the three athletes.

A rising star in women's soccer, Brianna Pinto was selected to speak at FIFA Congress on behalf of the United States. Right away, she formed a connection with Davies and Diego Lainez, the youth international player who spoke for Mexico.

All three of them were born in 2000. They were the next generation of soccer stars. They came from entirely different backgrounds. But now they were here, in Russia, unified towards a common goal.

"I think that's my favourite thing about soccer," Pinto said. "There are so many opportunities that it brings on the field, but the experiences off the field and the unlikely relationships you build through the game are what makes it special. It was so, so special to be a part of that bid."

For her part, Pinto had to submit a video to U.S. Soccer earlier in the year as part of their selection process. Unlike Davies and Lainez, Pinto won't be able to participate in the 2026 World Cup, but she still had a compelling story to share.

In her speech, she spoke about being the only girl on her teams growing up.

"The boys didn't mind," she said, "because I scored most of the goals."

She also spoke about playing against Iran's U-19 national team, just the second time the U.S. had faced Iran in women's soccer at any level.

"Moments like that have taught me, we may come from different countries and cultures, but deep down, we're all pretty much the same," she said, reiterating the "Football for All" message.

Pinto, Davies, and Lainez were almost inseparable throughout the trip. Although most of their time was spent rehearsing, they also found some moments to just be kids.

Like the time they bumped into Roberto Carlos at the Expocentre.

"We were going down an escalator and Alphonso's like, 'Hey, look!'" said Huoseh, who travelled to Russia with Davies and was involved in the planning process. "I go, 'What, man?'"

"It's Roberto Carlos!" Huoseh remembered him saying.

"What?"

"Yeah, yeah, yeah, he's right there!" Davies responded.

He ran down the escalator. Huoseh chased after him. Pinto and Lainez followed suit.

"It's Roberto Carlos!" Davies reiterated. "Best left foot in the world!"

Roberto Carlos, a legendary Brazilian left back who won the World Cup in 2002 and spent more than a decade with Spanish powerhouse Real Madrid, was one of many footballing icons in the building. Others included Cafu, Iker Casillas, Luís Figo, Diego Forlán, and Clarence Seedorf, whom they also met.

Ironically, Roberto Carlos was there as an ambassador for Morocco's bid. At any rate, he graciously accepted the request to take a photo with a star-struck Davies and his new friends.

"Here he is, he was going to go give his speech, he was really composed, but then you see the little kid in him come out," Huoseh said. "He's like, 'Oh my god!'"

The little kid in him came out the next day too.

Mexican Football Federation president Decio de María promised the trio of young stars that they'd be able to attend Mexico's training session if North America's bid was successful. They were especially excited to see Javier Hernández, better known as Chicharito, and Giovani dos Santos up close and personal in advance of their opening match against Germany.

"We were all super amped up," Pinto said. "It was so cool."

Later that evening, they rushed back to Moscow to attend the opening match of the tournament, between Russia and Saudi Arabia, alongside nearly 80,000 rabid spectators.

"It was just surreal," Pinto said. "I was like, we are in Russia, at a World Cup match, in a packed stadium. It was even better because Russia won 5–0, so the fans were going crazy."

As powerful as Davies's speech was, Pinto said it was these moments that gave her a true appreciation of the type of person he was. Whether it was chasing down Roberto Carlos on an escalator, cracking jokes and coming up with fun handshakes, or being giddy in the stands like a kid in a candy store, Pinto quickly learned that Davies wasn't your typical superstar.

"I think that's what sets him apart from other athletes," she said. "He's got personality, he's got love for life, and he's got so much appreciation for everyone that played a role in all his success."

That summer, his success was plentiful. That summer, his life changed forever.

Heading into the 2018 season, the Whitecaps acquired striker Kei Kamara to help bolster their attack.

Kamara, 33 at the time, had more than a decade's worth of experience in MLS and was one of the league's top goalscorers of all time. He'd also spent some time playing at the highest level in England and had a similar background to Davies, having escaped the civil war in Sierra Leone before moving to the United States as a refugee and becoming a naturalized citizen.

"It was a big brother, little brother kind of thing," Kamara said of his relationship with Davies. "It wasn't like a project where they said come in and mentor Phonzie, but we clicked right away."

Kamara remembered one of the first conversations he had with Davies. It was during the preseason on a team run at Pacific Spirit Regional Park, a forest trail just a skip and a hop away from the Whitecaps training facility at the University of British Columbia.

At that point, Kamara had heard about Davies. The hype was starting to grow. But he wanted to learn more. So he approached him during the run and struck up a conversation.

Or at least tried to.

"Hey, how have you been doing?" Kamara asked.

"Good," he remembered Davies saying.

"You've started a lot of games, I've heard about you. How many goals have you had in this league?"

"None," Davies responded, to Kamara's surprise.

"How many assists?"

"One."

"Wait, so what's all this hype about you?" Kamara joked. "Alright, we gotta change that."

"That" being the lack of production and the one-word answers, of course.

From then on, Davies and Kamara became inseparable. They would go out for African food. They roomed together on the road. On one trip to Minnesota, Kamara introduced Davies to the city's Liberian community. Davies would often spend time at Kamara's house, interacting with his young kids.

"He didn't come over to hang out with me. He came over to hang out with the kids," Kamara said. "When I'm hanging out with him, I'm giving him so many fricking life lessons.

"I remember a couple times, like once in LA, he was basically my third child with the kids and pushing the stroller coming through the airport. I remember me and my wife were walking, I actually forgot about the kids, and he was there. I just looked back and told my wife, 'This kid is just so good.'"

Kamara could see that Davies had personality. He was funny. He had spunk. He liked dancing. But he could also see that he was holding some of that back and not truly expressing himself when he wasn't around other people his age.

"I saw the fun in him locked up in a box," Kamara recalled. "Being in the position he's been in from 15 and jumping into the professional game, he didn't want to disrespect anyone. I think that's the African part in him, too, the respect when he's around older people."

That's where Kamara's "bad influence," as he jokingly put it, came into play.

In addition to scoring goals, Kamara is best known around MLS circles for his vibrant personality and unique goal celebrations. Sometimes, it rubbed people the wrong way and got him into trouble. On one occasion, he was shown a yellow card for twerking after a goal. But Kamara has never been afraid to put himself out there — whether it was on the field, on social media, or in any other setting — and it's something he encouraged Davies to do as well.

"I need you to be the fun guy, I need your social media to be popping, because guess what? There are so many kids that are following you in Canada right now," Kamara would tell him. "You have a personality, don't be shy to use it."

"Look at me," he continued. "People might be saying all this stuff, blah blah blah, but when I'm on the field, I have fun. When I get off the field, I fricking have fun. Those are some of the things I was trying to plug into him. Just let go."

In the very first game they played together, the Whitecaps won 2–1. Kamara scored the first goal, assisted by Davies. And Davies scored the second. They broke out into dance after both of them, including a "Wakanda Forever" tribute in reference to *Black Panther*.

"I think Phonzie has a dance partner now," Carl Robinson told reporters after the match. "Kei's a character. A good character for Phonzie. And that's what we need."

Their choreographed goal celebrations would become regular occurrences.

Davies became more and more influential as the season went on. And his breakout match came on June 9, 2018, just a few days before his trip to Russia for FIFA Congress. The Whitecaps scored five goals, beating Orlando 5–2. And Davies was directly involved in four of them. He scored one goal himself, added three assists, and made some of Orlando's defenders look like pylons in the process.

Davies had his moments prior to that match against Orlando.

He made the highlight reels. He got the odd goal or assist. But that was his first truly dominant performance, and it deservingly earned him MLS Player of the Week honours.

"When he performs like that, there's no hiding him," Robinson told reporters after the match. "He'll be all over the TVs and all over the newspapers."

"Today was, a lot of people might say, the best game of his career so far," Kamara added. "And hopefully it's just the start."

Indeed, it was.

Not long after Davies's return from Russia, the Whitecaps had back-to-back matches against Chicago Fire and D.C. United. Normally, these would be two routine opponents. But this year was different, as both teams had world-renowned superstars on their rosters.

Chicago had Bastian Schweinsteiger, a World Cup winner for Germany and an FC Bayern Munich legend. And D.C. had Wayne Rooney, the all-time leading goalscorer for both England and Manchester United.

These were two of the biggest names in world football, let alone MLS. Two of the best to have played the game for their respective countries. When they played, people paid attention. Including, as it turned out, Bayern Munich, who were negotiating with the Whitecaps in the midst of these very matches.

Davies took full advantage.

Against Chicago, he had the game-winning assist with one of his patented runs down the left wing, which had become his primary position. Following the match, the Whitecaps sent a communications intern down to the away locker room to collect quotes for media and interview Schweinsteiger for a video they were preparing related to Davies's inclusion in the upcoming MLS All-Star Game.

Schweinsteiger didn't know much about him, but there was this one comment that made the rounds and added to the hype that was rapidly building.

"How old is he?" Schweinsteiger asked.

"Seventeen," the intern responded.

"Oh, 17. He doesn't have his driver's licence, right?" Schweinsteiger chuckled. "Obviously, he has potential. If he keeps working, of course he probably has a chance to play in Europe. With that speed, that technique, the skills, if he works hard also for the defence, of course, he can play in Europe."

That night against Chicago, it was the speed.

The following week, against D.C., it was the skills. There was a lot of hype around that game in particular. Not only was it going to be Rooney's first match in MLS, it was also going to be the first match at Audi Field, a shiny new soccer-specific stadium in Washington, D.C.

On the eve of that game, Davies got together with Pinto and her family. Having met her at FIFA Congress a month prior, Davies knew Pinto lived in North Carolina and figured she might be interested in making the trip. Pinto also had family in Northern Virginia, only minutes away from Washington, so they knew the area well. They drove Davies around and showed him various landmarks, including the White House and Audi Field.

The world will be watching tomorrow's game, Pinto's parents told him.

"They were kind of planting that seed," Pinto said.

Afterwards, they went for dinner. As the guest, Davies got to choose the cuisine.

He was feeling burgers, so they went to Shake Shack.

"We can't get him Shake Shack!" Pinto told her dad.

"My dad's like, 'He's 17, let him eat out, he knows what he likes to eat!'" she laughed. "I mean, he balled out the next day, so I guess the Shake Shack helped?"

Whatever works.

In the final minute of the game, Davies scored a jaw-dropping goal in which he somehow tiptoed through four defenders who had him surrounded at the top right corner of the box before unleashing an "absolute wonder-strike," as the commentator called it. The Whitecaps were losing 3–0. The result wasn't in question. But for Davies, it was quite the consolation prize.

Heck, it might have been destiny.

A pair of conversations Davies had leading up to that moment certainly lend themselves to that theory. The first came with Pinto's parents at dinner the night before.

A burger joint by day, Shake Shack became a quasi-tactical war room that night.

"They were like, 'If you don't get any looks at goal on the left side, in the last 10 minutes of the game, switch to the right side because you can cut in with your left foot and hit it back post,'" Pinto recalled of the advice from her parents, who were both varsity athletes at North Carolina. "So we're in the stands at the game, having the time of our lives. Obviously it didn't go Vancouver's way, but he switched to the right side, he beat two or three players and bent it back post. I think that was one of the best goals in his career so far. It was so cool to see everything take off from there."

Never afraid to speak his mind, Kamara also pulled Davies aside and offered a few words of encouragement minutes before he scored.

"I went to him and said, 'Hey, we're having a shitty game. I just need you to do something. It's not about us anymore. The summer is here. It's about you. People are watching you,'" Kamara told Davies, referencing the summer transfer window, which typically involves a flurry of player movement around the soccer world. "You saw my reaction when he scored the goal, behind the leg, brought it back, and then just banged it. I was just like, 'Oh yeah.'"

The goal went viral on social media.

Partly because it came during Rooney's much-anticipated MLS debut and the christening of D.C. United's new stadium. Partly because it was the last goal Davies scored, and the last game he played, before reports of an imminent transfer leaked the following week. But mostly because it was a thing of beauty.

Some headlines following the goal called him the "wonderkid."

That summer, the world learned his name.

His name is Alphonso Davies.

CHAPTER 7:
THE TRANSFER

It was at the Edmonton International Airport, of all places, that Bayern Munich got the final signature they needed to secure, in their words, "one of football's most sought-after young talents."

Late that Monday night, the Bayern brain trust met Davies's parents for the first time. This was far from a formal meeting. They greeted in the baggage claim area, steps away from Tim Hortons. After some handshakes and pleasantries, everyone made their way upstairs.

Seated in plain sight on a couple of seats next to the airport's observation area, Bayern sporting director Hasan Salihamidžić laid out all the documents for Davies's parents to review. Since Davies was still a minor, he needed a guardian to co-sign. If this was in Europe, it probably would have been a circus. But this wasn't Munich. This wasn't Madrid.

This was Edmonton, Alberta.

None of the passersby blinked an eye. Right then and there, in the unlikeliest of locations, the then-richest transfer in MLS history was consummated.

"His mom and dad just looked at me and said, 'Oh, thank you, habibi," Huoseh recalled, referencing the Arabic word "my love" or "darling" commonly used as an affectionate nickname. "It was so fast. It was in and out. It was like, I don't know, 10 or 11 o'clock at night. They were just going through the motions. I don't think it even absorbed at that time."

It was a whirlwind for everyone involved.

In less than 24 hours, Davies and the group working on the transfer would travel from one end of the continent to the other with stops in five different cities — starting in Vancouver, followed by the impromptu pit stop in Edmonton, a red-eye to Newark via Toronto, and finally a 90-minute shuttle to Philadelphia, where Davies would undergo a medical the next morning.

Conveniently, Bayern was already in Philadelphia for their annual U.S. tour, so their doctors and trainers were able to examine Davies there for any red flags. That wasn't a formality, either. Rather, it was a two-day process that included a myriad of tests at the Pennsylvania Hospital, where Bayern used a fake name for Davies to avoid tipping off the media, and at the team's hotel. With millions of dollars at play, they needed to know if there was any risk on their investment.

Finally, once the medical, photo ops, and interviews were complete, Huoseh and Davies took a moment to appreciate where they were — and where Davies was headed.

In Huoseh's hotel room at the Ritz-Carlton, Philadelphia, where Bayern had set up shop for the trip, he put his hands on Davies's shoulders and said, "Man, I'm so proud of you. You're here. Look at you. You're going to one of the biggest clubs in the world."

"Coach, you crying?" he remembered Davies responding.

He was, in fact, a bit teary-eyed.

After all, this was the same kid he used to drive all around Edmonton for games and practices, the same kid that used to come over to his house and hang out with his son for hours on end.

The same kid.

"He kind of just gave me a hug," Huoseh said. "It was a very touching moment."

As coined by the *Edmonton Sun*, Huoseh is the "Accidental Agent."

His background is in electrical engineering. Before jumping into soccer full-time, he ran a successful company in the Edmonton area, ASI Tech, that built communications infrastructure for the oil and gas sector, among others. Many of his views on life are shaped by his father, a Palestinian who came to Canada as a refugee after being exiled from his home.

"He went through all these hardships," Huoseh said. "And he's a simple guy. He always used to tell us, when you're sitting with elitists, people with wealth or whatever, people who think they're high class, don't ever lower your head in front of them. Don't ever feel belittled. And he said when you're sitting with people who don't have much, who are simple, who are humble, be at their level. Don't try to belittle people like that. Always be fair. Connecting with Alphonso's family, to me they're just human beings who were put through a hardship in their life and ended up here. They're good people."

In those early days, Debeah and Victoria would often go to Huoseh for advice. When the Whitecaps came calling, he helped navigate the process. Eventually, though, it became clear that Davies needed an agent. So the Whitecaps provided some recommendations. Huoseh looked into a few others.

In total, he said there were "half a dozen or so" options on the table. Huoseh and Davies even flew to New York to meet with Roc Nation Sports, the agency founded by Jay-Z.

"I was just going through the process and I guess you could say interviewing and trying to figure out which one of them would be the best fit for Alphonso," Huoseh said. "Some of them were sending him soccer boots or whatever. So I put a bunch of stuff together, some of the proposals I got, and I went and sat with his family. I said, 'Look, we need to get him an agent. There are other things happening. People are calling about doing marketing deals. He's doing really well in MLS; there are going to be big opportunities for this kid.'"

As he sat with Debeah and Victoria in their apartment, Huoseh started going through the documents. A lot of it was legal jargon. He remembered getting through a single page before Victoria intervened.

"Nick, habibi, why don't you just do this?" Huoseh recalled her saying.

"I said, 'Look, I'm worried that I'll make a mistake,'" he responded. "This is just not my industry. My tech company was really busy. I was doing really well there."

"We'd *rather* you do this," they explained.

Debeah and Victoria knew Huoseh was educated. They knew he dealt with contracts at work. He knew this was a different beast, but they insisted.

So Huoseh checked with Davies. He was on board too.

"I said, 'OK, you guys have to be patient with me,'" Huoseh recalled.

He notified the Whitecaps and the other agents who were interested. Everyone was taken aback. Some of the agents scoffed at the decision.

"None of us were born into our professions," Huoseh thought. "Everybody learns as they go."

And he had to learn *fast*.

Huoseh had heard the whispers about European interest in Davies very early on. As the Whitecaps academy director who often travelled overseas for various conferences and coaching courses, Craig Dalrymple had as well. His counterparts would always ask for intel.

He had a stock answer.

"It's a no-risk investment," he would tell them. "There's nothing to suggest he can't hit the top level. And most importantly, his character is so genuine and true."

In the spring of 2017, MLS arranged for Dalrymple and his peers throughout the league to visit some clubs in Spain and France as part of an education program in partnership with La Liga, Spain's top league. One of the stops was La Liga's headquarters in Madrid.

Dalrymple typically sat in the front row for any talks or presentations.

"My eyesight is not the best," he joked.

During one talk, a high-ranking La Liga official was speaking to the group about how clubs worked together with the national association to identify top talents when he stopped mid-track and pointed to Dalrymple, who was wearing his Whitecaps polo.

"Alphonso Davies, top prospect in the world right now," the official announced.

"I remember calling the club that night and saying, 'Hey, just so you know, this is what I've heard from a La Liga director,'" Dalrymple said. "That's when the penny really dropped for me. Unsolicited, this individual, who was in a top position in one of the top five leagues in the world, would identify Alphonso at that time as a top prospect in the world."

A few months later, following Davies's breakout performance with the Canadian national team at the 2017 Concacaf Gold Cup, a French club flew to Vancouver and began to show some "real interest," according to former Whitecaps vice-president of soccer operations Greg Anderson. Not long after, he said, the Whitecaps received their first formal offer for Davies from a separate club.

It wouldn't be the last.

Publicly, the first big European clubs linked to Davies were Liverpool and Manchester United, which so happen to be the two most successful clubs in English Premier League history. As far as the most popular sports franchises in the world go, they're usually near the top of the list.

With Liverpool, there was a connection through former Whitecaps defender Andy O'Brien. After parting ways with the Whitecaps following the 2014 season, O'Brien hung up his boots and returned to the United Kingdom, where he became a scout for Liverpool.

Based in his hometown, Harrogate, O'Brien was primarily focused on the UK region but also tracked players in MLS, kept in touch with some of his former Whitecaps teammates, and followed the team's progress. Back in 2016, O'Brien said the first thing he did every Sunday morning was check how the Whitecaps had fared the night before.

That fall, O'Brien made a trip back to Vancouver for the Whitecaps charity alumni match and saw Davies play in person. Coincidentally, he was in attendance for Davies's first MLS start.

He also travelled to Wales at the beginning of 2017 to watch Davies and the Whitecaps play some preseason friendlies against UK-based U-23 teams. There, he was joined by other European scouts that Carl Robinson had invited from teams like Swansea City, Crystal Palace, and Rosenborg.

Davies dazzled in a 4–0 win over Bristol City, scoring two goals, and O'Brien had a front-row seat. Truth be told, he was standing. The match was played on a field at the hotel resort next to a literal castle. There were no seats.

"Liverpool were one of the first clubs to actually come here and physically scout him," Whitecaps president Bob Lenarduzzi told local radio station TSN 1040 in July 2018. "It was Andy O'Brien who was tasked with watching him. I know he was very impressed and I think he made a recommendation that they should make a move."

It was a similar story with Manchester United.

Jorge Alvial joined the Red Devils as an international scout in 2016, the same year Davies broke onto the scene in Vancouver. Prior to that, he'd spent nearly a decade with Chelsea.

At both clubs, Alvial was responsible for scouting North, Central, and South America. He scouted and recommended some of the world's very best players at a young age, including Neymar, James Rodríguez, Alexis Sánchez, and yes, Alphonso Davies.

Alvial saw Davies play for the first time when he was 14 years old and still a member of the Edmonton Strikers. It was during the 2015 Dallas Cup, which, if you recall, was the same trip where Davies's coaches found him alone in the gym after a marathon travel day.

"I saw him and I liked him because he was fast," said Alvial, who was in between the Chelsea and Manchester United jobs at the time. "He was playing against a Mexican team. You could see the level of technique of the Mexican team was way above the Canadian team. But he made a difference because of his speed. I saw him there for one game and then I kept watching different ones."

He did make a note of Davies, however.

And the following year, when Alvial started working for Manchester United, he did so again. This time, it was Alvial's son Javier who brought Vancouver's number 67 to his attention.

Javier was a former professional player who would later become the manager of scouting and recruitment for the Portland Timbers. At the time, he was an assistant scout to his father and tasked with sifting through video footage of various United Soccer League matches. There were three players that caught his eye.

So he passed them along to his father.

"One guy, OK good, the other guy, good, and the other one, 'Wow, I like that guy,'" Alvial said, realizing the same player he saw a year ago was now making his mark as a professional. "I told him, 'You know what, next game I'm going to go see him.'

"I called Man U and said, 'Listen, I want to go to Vancouver.' And I flew. What I saw was a 15-year-old boy that could beat a 25-year-old boy with his speed. And not just beat him, but blow by him . . . Right away I made a report to my superior and I said, 'We *have* to get this kid.'"

Alvial, who was based in Atlanta, said he made at least seven trips to see Davies play. He had the same reaction every time. He knew the longer Manchester United waited to make a move, the more likely it was that other teams would get involved.

And that's exactly what happened.

"Someone put something on the MLS website or a newspaper somewhere, I saw my name, watching Alphonso Davies," Alvial recalled. "Then you started to see the scouts. And every time I went to see him, I would say hi to all the other scouts, because I knew they were there."

He remembered speaking to a counterpart from rival club Manchester City who "had his doubts" about Davies. He also remembered an occasion where a Bayern scout jokingly came and sat right next to him.

"I told him, 'He's very slow so you shouldn't be here,'" Alvial laughed.

On one of his first trips to Vancouver, Alvial arranged a meeting with Davies through Huoseh. If this was a player he was recommending, he wanted to know the person too.

"So I asked him, 'What would you do if you started making $200,000?'" Alvial recalled. "And he said, 'Well, my first paycheque I'd be saving because I want to buy my mother a car.' What kid thinks like that? The good kids. The other ones are thinking, 'I'm saving money because I want to buy a car for myself.' And then he said, 'If I ever make it big, I want to buy them a home.'"

Then Davies explained a little bit of his family's background. Alvial could relate, having moved to the U.S. as a 14-year-old to escape the dictatorship in his native Chile. That conversation only reaffirmed his belief in Davies's potential, but his recommendations fell on deaf ears. It's not that Manchester United didn't have any interest. They were just hesitant to pull the trigger.

Interestingly, their academy director, Nicky Butt, and U-23 head coach, Warren Joyce, were both on the same UEFA Pro coaching course as Dalrymple that ran concurrently with Davies's two and a half years in MLS. His name inevitably came up in many of their conversations.

"It was 'We know about him, we're tracking him, we have serious interest in him,'" Dalrymple recalled.

They even invited Davies to join the club on a three-week training stint as arranged by Huoseh following the 2017 season. But the Whitecaps denied the request, citing the need for Davies to get a mental and physical break over the holidays.

As time went on, Alvial grew impatient.

"Believe me, I was a pain at Man U," he said. "They didn't want to hear me that much. They couldn't accept or imagine that I could be speaking so highly of a Canadian or American kid."

At one point, he even went above his boss and wrote directly to José Mourinho, Manchester United's coach at the time. Mourinho is one of the game's most decorated coaches, and Alvial already had a relationship with him from their time together at Chelsea.

"This boy has what it takes," Alvial remembered Mourinho saying.

Then things started to get more serious.

He figured it was too late.

Michael Reschke was sitting in his office at the VfB Stuttgart headquarters when his phone rang.

It wasn't the news he wanted.

A top-flight club in Germany, Stuttgart had been tracking Davies for three or four months. One of their scouts had gone to see him on multiple occasions. And Reschke, who was the club's sporting director, had reviewed a one-hour video package made up entirely of Davies game footage.

"It was outstanding what we saw in the video," Reschke said, adding that Davies moved "like a fish in the water" when he was on the field. "It was a little bit crazy what we saw."

In the context of world soccer, Stuttgart isn't a big spender. If they're going to spend big bucks, it has to be on a player who can contribute right away, Reschke said.

It was a little bit of a risk with Davies, but they felt he could do just that.

"We discussed it with our financial department and we agreed that we'd be able to spend eight or nine million euro for the transfer," Reschke said. "But that was the highest amount that was possible for us."

So Reschke sent his "right-hand man," Joachim Cast, to Vancouver to meet with Huoseh and open discussions. Then he got a call from Cast that he still agonizes over to this day.

"Marco Neppe is also here," Cast told him.

"No, that cannot be true," he responded in disbelief.

Neppe was the chief scout for Bayern Munich. In fact, Reschke was the one who had brought him there. They had worked hand in hand up until Reschke left his post as Bayern's technical director to take the job at Stuttgart just one year prior.

If Neppe was in Vancouver, Reschke knew exactly what that meant.

"We were out of the game," he said.

Historically, Stuttgart has been one of the most respected clubs in Germany. But they're not in the same class as Bayern Munich, the undisputed giants of the region.

Not many are.

If Bayern wants a player, more often than not they get him. And they certainly wanted Davies — essentially from the moment they laid eyes on him.

"It was like, 'What is this?'" Neppe said when asked about his first impressions of Davies. "'What kind of speed? What kind of quick feet?' It was like there's somebody flying.

"The profile was really amazing and exceptional. It was the mix between the technical skills — the quick feet, the speed with the ball — and then he was really sharp [without] the ball . . . For us, it was a joy to watch him and follow him. The belief and how we were convinced about him: it was a process of days, not weeks."

The process of signing him wasn't as straightforward.

Neppe said it was UK-based agent Neil Sang, who'd been working with Huoseh to look at opportunities for Davies in Europe, who initially contacted him regarding the young Canadian. But to move things forward and ensure he was speaking to the appropriate parties, Neppe decided to reach out to an old teammate who happened to be in Vancouver.

"You never know who's the right agent and how you can get in touch with the right person, so it was like, hmm, how should I do [this]?" Neppe recalled. "For me, in that case, it was really special because the goalkeeper of the Vancouver Whitecaps in that moment was Stefan Marinovic. And I played with him in Wiesbaden in my own active career."

So Neppe sent Marinovic a message via social media, establishing a connection with the Whitecaps, and discussions took off.

"He gave me the number of the coach, Carl Robinson," Neppe said. "Then I was in touch with the coach. And one day later, I was in touch with Greg Anderson."

From there, Neppe said there were "a lot of nights on the phone" with the Whitecaps as they engaged in negotiations over the span of two to three weeks.

"And it was always difficult because of the time difference," he said. "My wife in that time was saying, 'Hey, why are you awake between one and four o'clock in the [morning]?' I said, 'There's a player in Canada. I have to invest all my time for this guy.'"

By the summer of 2018, Bayern was one of "probably a dozen clubs" pursuing Davies, according to Huoseh. Top clubs, too, from countries like Germany, England, Spain, and France.

Stuttgart, of course, was one of them.

Manchester United was still in the running.

Arsenal was "very, very keen," according to Robinson, who had some teams reach out to him for an assessment of Davies as a person and player.

Barcelona had interest — though it was for their reserve team, Barcelona B, rather than the Spanish La Liga superpower that featured Davies's childhood idol, Lionel Messi.

And there were others.

It all came to a head at the end of July, when news broke that Bayern was in advanced talks with the Whitecaps and had travelled to Vancouver to seal the deal.

"When we knew Bayern was interested enough to fly, we gave all the other clubs a bit of a deadline to say look, 'We're going to meet with another club on this date, so if you're serious, come to us with an offer before this date,'" Anderson recalled, confirming the Whitecaps received 8 to 10 genuine offers.

Once that date passed, Anderson said, the Whitecaps paused the other conversations. But that wasn't the end of it. Different agents and clubs kept coming out of the woodwork, calling Anderson, Huoseh, and others that were close to Davies.

"I remember people calling me saying, 'Can I speak to him, can I get to him?'" Kei Kamara recalled. "I was like, 'No, I'm not his agent. You don't call me to try and talk to him.'"

One club even offered to sign Huoseh's son to their youth team as an incentive. It was non-stop right up until the day Davies was going to sign with Bayern, when another club made a last-minute pitch.

The class of Ligue 1 in France. Home to Neymar and Kylian Mbappé.

Paris Saint-Germain.

"They contacted me and said, 'We want to fly out to Vancouver, we're coming in. We'd like for you to hold up and meet with us,'" Huoseh recalled. "I said, 'Listen, guys, I'll be honest with you, don't bother coming out. We're already going to sign with Bayern, I think we're going to move forward with this.'"

After training that Monday, Davies asked Pa-Modou Kah for a ride to the meeting with Bayern, which was going to be held at the Hyatt Regency Vancouver.

"I'm not a cheap taxi," Kah joked.

At that point, Kah had retired as a player and was a staff coach within the Whitecaps organization. He had a lot of contacts from his time in Europe. Davies trusted him. They talked about everything. And they were in the car together when Kah got a call from PSG's sporting director, Antero Henrique.

"I put him on loudspeaker, so that Phonzie knows," Kah said. "I'm like, 'My dude, the guy is sitting here about to go into a meeting with Bayern Munich. They're here. So you guys want to come in one or two days, maybe the deal is done. Sorry, I'm not going to tell this kid not to take a deal. We're talking about Bayern Munich. We're not talking about a small club.'"

If they were serious, Kah told them to "put an offer onto the table." If nothing else, he figured that would help drive up the price.

Kah felt some people had the "wrong idea" of what he was doing. He said all he wanted was the best for Davies, for him to have all the information, and most importantly for him to get what he wanted.

In the end, that was Bayern Munich.

As with any transaction of this nature, the first step was for the two clubs to agree on a transfer fee. Davies was still under contract with the Whitecaps, so Bayern needed to pay them a sum of money to essentially acquire his rights. Unlike most North American sports leagues, where swaps of players and/or draft picks are the norm, transfers in the soccer world typically revolve around dollars and cents.

A lot of them.

Determining Davies's value wasn't an exact science, however. He was clearly a blue-chip prospect, but he was Canadian. And he was playing in MLS.

That complicated things.

MLS was on the rise, but it was understood to have weaker competition than Europe's top leagues and didn't have much of a history producing top young talent.

In one of his earliest reports to Manchester United, Alvial said he estimated that Davies's value would have been around US$2 to $3 million. Previously, the biggest outgoing transfer from MLS was reportedly US$10 million, when New York Red Bulls sold Jozy Altidore to Spanish club Villarreal CF in 2008.

This is peanuts compared to some of the cash that gets thrown around amongst the top dogs in Europe. PSG, for example, had just completed an unprecedented spending spree in which they doled out close to a half a billion dollars to land Neymar from Barcelona and Mbappé from AS Monaco FC in the two most expensive transfers of all time.

In the end, the Whitecaps and Bayern came to an agreement on a "fixed transfer fee and additional compensation that could total more than US$22 million, the most ever received by an MLS club in the league's 23-year history," the Whitecaps confirmed in their press release. The base transfer fee was in the region of US$13.5 million, nevertheless eclipsing the previous MLS record.

"The difference between the first offer and the final offer, and maybe I'm saying too much, there's a significant difference," Lenarduzzi said in the press conference announcing the deal. "When it comes to that, it's a bit like gambling. Do you take the early offers? Do you wait for others to come in?

"It took three weeks and throughout the process, the interest got better and better. It also helps that Alphonso was doing what he was doing on the pitch. And that happened just recently. The game that he scored the token goal [against D.C. United], it was a pretty good token goal, and it made highlight reels all over the place. I think a number of things need to come together to get the best deal possible."

When Neppe saw the goal against D.C. United, he thought to himself, "OK, that's some more euros." But at that point, it didn't even matter. Bayern was laser-focused.

They were going to get their guy.

Davies didn't receive a share of the transfer fee — the Whitecaps asked his representatives to waive the 10 percent he was technically entitled to, as per the MLS Collective Bargaining Agreement. It was explained this was common practice in MLS and an amount Davies could try to recoup in the form of a signing bonus or a salary bump since it was all part of Bayern's investment. But the ask still left a "sour taste," Huoseh said, feeling Davies had earned that money, which would have set the family up for success much earlier. And it provided the backdrop as Davies and his representatives opened discussions with Bayern on his own contract.

This was the final step.

Bayern sent Salihamidžić, one of the highest-profile decision-makers at the club, to Vancouver alongside Neppe and director of legal affairs Michael Gerlinger. They met with Davies and his representatives at the Whitecaps' offices on the fifth floor of the Landing, a heritage building just steps away from the famous Gastown Steam Clock. It was a sunny Sunday morning, so the streets were lively. Inside, the offices were more or less deserted. They set up in the boardroom, overlooking the stunning Vancouver Harbour, where Bayern's top brass would make their pitch.

Salihamidžić and Neppe laid out their plan for Davies in a slick PowerPoint presentation.

They explained the makeup of their roster. The legendary attacking duo of Arjen Robben and Franck Ribéry, affectionately nicknamed "Robbery," were both moving on at the end of the season after 10-plus years with the club. They were both wingers, just like Davies. Bayern already carried a thin roster. And now there would be even more space for Davies to come in and get an opportunity.

They illustrated where Davies might fit in on the field. At the time, they were experimenting with the idea of a 3-5-2 formation, which would allow Davies to use his speed along the left wing as a wingback — a position designed for athletic players who can run up and down the outside of the field to serve as both a defender and an attacker. But they showed a few different formations with Davies slotted in.

And they assured Davies that he would be a first-team player. In many instances, a big club will buy a young talent only to send them on loan elsewhere or let them simmer on the reserve team for years. And Huoseh said that it likely would have been the case with some clubs he spoke to, particularly in England, due to the high threshold for foreigners to obtain a work permit in the UK. But Bayern "never once" mentioned the possibility of a loan.

No other club presented a plan as detailed as this one.

"The other clubs I spoke to, it was just talk," Huoseh said.

Bayern had done their research on Davies. They'd seen his social media, his "dancing skills," and the "positive energy" he exuded, Neppe said. And they were expecting to get a glimpse of that during the meeting. But much to their surprise, he barely said a word.

"He was like a poker face," Neppe recalled. "He was sitting beside his agents and it was like, huh? Why is he not making jokes? Why is he not speaking too much? We showed him a video and explained

Davies was born on the Buduburam refugee camp in Ghana, where his family found safe haven amidst the Liberian civil war.

He was five years old when the family immigrated to Canada.

Top row (left to right): Davies's father, Debeah; sister, Angel; and mother, Victoria. Bottom row (left to right): Davies's brother, Bryan; and Davies.

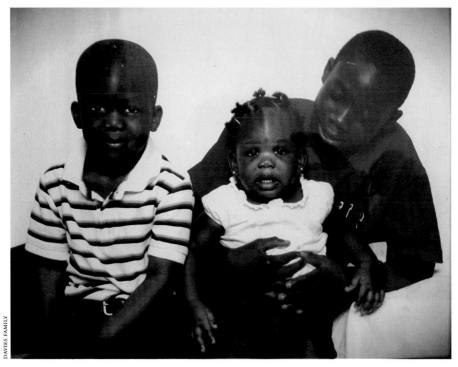

As a young child, Davies would often babysit Bryan and Angel while his parents were working.

"He was always a step ahead of everyone on the field."
— Nedal Huoseh, Davies's agent and former Strikers coach

Davies began playing organized soccer at nine years old with Edmonton Internazionale Soccer Club, or Inter SC, before joining the Edmonton Strikers (pictured).

"He had it as a goal that he was going to work hard every day, train every day, and get better."
— Talal Al-Awaid, former Strikers coach

With the Strikers, Davies was usually deployed in the middle of the park as an attacking midfielder with the freedom to roam.

He wore number 10 — commonly reserved for the most creative or offensively gifted player on the team.

In 2012, Davies joined the soccer academy at St. Nicholas Catholic Junior High School in Edmonton's Beverly Heights neighbourhood. As a Grade 7 student playing with and against students who were mostly in Grades 8 and 9, he was usually one of the youngest players on the field.

"The truth is we get all kinds of athletes with exceptional athleticism. The thing that separated Alphonso from the rest was his technique on the ball that coincided with his athleticism. That was rare."

— Marco Bossio, St. Nicholas Soccer Academy director

In Grade 8, he was named team captain — despite still being one of the youngest players.

St. Nicholas won the city championship in each of the three years Davies was there.

Davies joined the Vancouver Whitecaps youth academy in August 2015, a few months before his 15th birthday.

At 15 years, eight months, and 15 days, he became the second youngest player to appear in an MLS game.

Within his first couple years as a professional, Davies would become the youngest goalscorer in the history of the Whitecaps, United Soccer League, Canadian Championship, Canadian men's national team, Concacaf Champions League, and Concacaf Gold Cup.

It wasn't until March 4, 2018, however, that he scored his first goal in Major League Soccer.

Davies and his "dancing partner," Kei Kamara, developed a special bond during their one season together in Vancouver.

Davies put on a show in his first game following the Bayern transfer announcement, scoring two breathtaking goals and adding two assists.

"With all the big news going on, coming back to Vancouver, I wanted it to be special."
— Alphonso Davies

Catch him if you can. Davies hit a top speed of 37.8 km/h during his time in Vancouver, according to Whitecaps head of physical preparation Jon Poli.

Davies's family was flown into town for his final game with the Whitecaps on October 28, 2018. It was marketed as the "Farewell Phonzie" send-off.

Fittingly, Davies scored both goals in a 2–1 win.

A minute of applause took place during the 67th minute — a nod to his jersey number.

He was subbed off to a standing ovation.

Following the game, Davies posed for a photo with Vancouver Canucks legends Henrik and Daniel Sedin and then-goaltender Jacob Markstrom.

Davies and his little brother, Bryan, with the official game ball.

After posting eight goals and 11 assists, Davies was voted the Whitecaps player of the year in his final season with the club.

Davies, 17, flew to Philadelphia to undergo a medical and complete his landmark transfer to Bayern Munich.

A warm welcome upon Davies's arrival in Munich.

In his first training session at Bayern, Davies walked onto the field with the legendary Arjen Robben. The "Jedi Master and his Padawan," as Bayern's North American Twitter account called the duo that day.

Davies won his first Bundesliga title in 2019. The first of many.

What dreams are made of: Davies against his idol, Lionel Messi, in the UEFA Champions League.

Davies was the first Canadian men's national team player to win the UEFA Champions League.

to him the roadmap, the plan we have, the project we want to start with him, and he was like, 'OK, uh huh.'"

"Phonzie, we've never met each other, but I love you," Neppe joked.

"OK, uh huh."

It was an overwhelming time for Davies, to say the very least, and according to Huoseh, he wasn't comfortable in these formal settings. So after viewing Bayern's presentation, he took off and let Huoseh and Sang handle the contract negotiations. Naturally, there was some back and forth. At the end of the meeting, Huoseh laid out the demands in no uncertain terms.

"They said, 'We can't do that,'" Huoseh recalled. "I said, 'OK, that's fine, then. Figure out what you can do, and let's meet tomorrow.' And I just packed up my stuff and left."

The next day, they agreed to terms on a four-and-a-half-year contract that would reportedly pay Davies around US$1 million per year — more than 10 times the $72,500 he'd been making previously. That Monday afternoon, Davies signed the papers in a conference room at the Hyatt, setting in motion the cross-continent trek to Philadelphia and a landmark announcement that made news all over the soccer world.

"You dream about this as a kid," Davies told Vancouver media upon his return.

"A lot of clubs showed interest, but they really wanted me and really put in the effort to get me," he said of Bayern. "Those are the guys as a kid I was looking up to, watching them on TV, playing with them in *FIFA*. Being able to meet them and being able to play on the team is exciting."

"Are there some nerves?" one reporter asked.

"Yeah, I'm a little bit nervous," Davies responded, "but life comes with challenges and I'm ready to take this one on."

CHAPTER 8:
FAREWELL PHONZIE

It was the most exhilarating week of his life. Probably the most exhausting too.

Having completed his medicals in Philadelphia, finalizing the much-anticipated transfer to Bayern Munich, Davies flew back to Vancouver late Wednesday.

And the Whitecaps had a game on Saturday.

FIFA's regulations state that a player is only able to officially transfer to a team in another country once they're 18 years old. Davies was still 17. So it was agreed upon that he would play out the rest of the season in Vancouver before moving to Germany.

His schedule that week looked something like this:

Sunday, July 22

- Meeting with Bayern in Vancouver

Monday, July 23

- Morning training session with the Whitecaps
- Second meeting with Bayern in Vancouver
- Evening flight to Edmonton
- Red-eye flight to Newark, via Toronto

Tuesday, July 24

- Early morning drive to Philadelphia
- Medicals and meetings with Bayern

Wednesday, July 25

- Complete medicals
- Interview and photos with Bayern content team
- Flight back to Vancouver

Thursday, July 26

- Morning training session with the Whitecaps
- Afternoon interviews with Vancouver media

Friday, July 27

- Morning training session with the Whitecaps

Saturday, July 28

- Gameday

Some observers wondered whether he'd need a mental break or more training time to get up to speed. It wasn't a guarantee that he'd start the match on Saturday, or even play at all. But Whitecaps fans were desperate to see their "Homegrown Hero" back in action — Davies had been held out of the last few matches as the transfer negotiations heated up.

Meanwhile, Bayern fans would have been equally as eager to get a first glimpse of their new prized signing, albeit from afar.

They both got their wish.

That Saturday night at BC Place, Davies scored two breathtaking goals, "golazos" as they say in soccer, and added two assists in a 4–2 win over Minnesota United FC.

"With all the big news going on, coming back to Vancouver, I wanted it to be special," Davies said after the match.

It sure was.

On the first goal, Davies faked a shot at the top of the box, dragged the ball around the hapless defender with the sole of his foot, took three additional touches to evade the other defenders chasing him down, and nutmegged the goalkeeper from close range.

Put it in the Louvre.

On the second goal, he split a pair of defenders that were approaching, skipped past a third one by bouncing the ball off the turf as he entered the penalty area, and fired a left-footed strike into the top corner.

Add it to the exhibit.

"After that transfer, and that game, and that special goal, taking how many guys on, I remember tackling the shit out of him," said Kei Kamara, the beneficiary of one of Davies's assists that evening. "I tackled him so hard on the ground. Just saying, 'Man, I can't believe I'm able to share the field with you.'"

"He had just signed for Bayern Munich, the whole footballing world is looking at him, and he comes out, two goals, two assists, some incredibly tight feet in tight spaces, made it look easy," Whitecaps co-owner and NBA legend Steve Nash said in a Whitecaps video. "He looked like he was playing with the U-15s. Not to disrespect anyone, that's just how good he is."

"He played one of the best games I've ever seen anyone play," Russell Teibert said in a video produced by MLS. "He was on fire. And you thought, 'OK, this kid's the real deal.'"

And so began his farewell tour in MLS.

For those next three months, Davies was the centre of attention everywhere he went. There were way more interviews. Way more autographs — lineups at the Whitecaps training facility, on occasion. And he was still trying to finish high school, help the Whitecaps sneak into the playoffs, and prepare for the move to Germany.

There would be no time for rest.

Just a week after returning from Philadelphia and days after his star showing vs. Minnesota, Davies participated in the 2018 MLS All-Star Game in Atlanta. He was the commissioner's pick, a personal selection by MLS commissioner Don Garber, joining other top players in MLS for the league's summer showcase.

The MLS All-Stars faced Juventus FC, the heavyweight of Italy's Serie A, in front of a whopping 72,317 fans at Mercedes-Benz Stadium. Davies showed his promise in a half-hour cameo but stole the show with some hilarious comments in a subsequent "mic'd up" video.

He joked with his teammates on the sideline.

"At the All-Star Game, ey, chillin' with Bradley Wright-Phillips, ey, he bring the flame, eyyy," he freestyled as Wright-Phillips and others erupted into laughter.

He gave a shout-out to Mom.

"I'm on TV," he said as he ran onto the field. "Momma, we made it!"

And, as usual, he showed his kid-like fandom.

"Yo, man, I have you on *FIFA*! You're OP," he told Juventus player Alex Sandro after the match, using a shorthand term from the video gaming community that means "overpowered."

The all-star game capped off a life-changing two months that included Davies's MLS Player of the Week performance vs. Orlando, the heartfelt speech to FIFA Congress in Russia, the highlight-reel goals and assists vs. D.C. and Chicago, and, of course, the transfer to Bayern and subsequent homecoming.

It was the summer of Phonzie. And he was enjoying every moment.

"He was happy during that time, because I think that he was realizing his dreams," Theo Bair said. "And he knew that he was making everyone around him proud. I remember I was Snapchatting him when he was at the all-star game. At the time, I hadn't played in the league at all, so I was a really big fan of Alberth Elis. And he was sitting with him. So Phonzie was sending me videos of Alberth saying hi to me, I was having little conversations with them.

"Phonzie was having the time of his life."

Davies played his final MLS match on October 28, 2018. With the Whitecaps already eliminated from playoff contention, it was marketed as the "Farewell Phonzie" send-off.

Davies's whole family was flown into town. And TSN had a video crew follow their every move for a TSN Original documentary, titled *Phonzie*.

Meanwhile, the Whitecaps had a videographer meet Davies the morning of the game and ride with him to the stadium for an "All Access" video. Davies drove in his white Volkswagen, having recently obtained his driver's licence.

Fans were encouraged to sign a giant postcard that would be presented to him.

The first 1,000 fans in the building got a Davies poster.

Video messages from various athletes and celebrities, including Edmonton Oilers superstars Connor McDavid and Leon Draisaitl and Canadian Olympic medalist Andre De Grasse, were shown on the scoreboard and on social media leading up to the match. A video message from Davies himself, thanking the fans of Vancouver, was shown too.

A minute of applause was arranged in the 67th minute — a nod to Davies's jersey number.

There was a lot going on.

"At that time, the pressure was so great on Alphonso," said Craig Dalrymple, Vancouver's interim head coach at the time. "Everyone wanted to speak to him, everyone wanted to see him play, everyone wanted a piece of his attention."

And there was some doubt that he was even going to play. Dalrymple said Davies had recently suffered an ankle twist, but one of his "superpowers" was his ability to recover from injury quickly.

He wasn't going to miss this game.

"I remember him coming to me the day before the game saying it's a lot, he needs people to leave him alone for a little bit, so he can focus on the game, get into his routine," Dalrymple said. "And the club was very good; it managed the requests and whatnot. His last training session I think was tough for him, but he got through it.

"And then the game itself, he did his thing."

The Whitecaps won 2–1. Davies scored both goals. Once again, he rose to the occasion.

He always did.

You could see what it meant to him as he celebrated the goals in each corner at the north end of the field. The pure emotion on his face was matched by the ecstasy of the crowd.

For Davies, it was a chance to give thanks to the city that took him in as a 14-year-old and the club that gave him an opportunity to realize his dream of becoming a professional soccer player.

"These have been the best three years of my life," he said in the video message shown prior to the match. "Every time I stepped on the field for this great club, I tried to give my all and play with a smile on my face. And you supported me, every single time. I heard you, every single time. You'll always be a part of my story. And now it's time for the next chapter. It's time to say goodbye."

For the city of Vancouver, it was a chance to salute their "Homegrown Hero" one last time. The pride and joy of the organization. The kid they saw become a superstar right in front of their eyes. The city fell in love with Davies. It was hard not to. After a game one night, he even called 911 to report a building on fire, potentially saving lives.

Yes, that actually happened.

During a time when their rivals were winning MLS Cups, Davies was their shining light.

With those two goals, he gave the fans his parting gift. Now it was their turn. A few minutes before the final whistle, Davies was subbed off to a deafening standing ovation.

"I was having a discussion with the coaches on the bench, like, 'What do I do? Do I pull him off?'" Dalrymple recalled. "He probably wants to get his hat-trick goal, and what a way that would be to finish. We're 2–1 up, I don't want to burst this balloon at all. I wanted it to be the right end for him. And then, of course, we had another Homegrown on the bench, Simon Colyn, that I wanted to try and get into the match. All the first-team players wanted him to play and get his first taste of it."

So Dalrymple decided to make the swap.

"Coach, I didn't want to come off," Dalrymple remembered Davies saying on the sideline.

"I said, 'I know. I know. But it was important for you to understand how much you mean to these fans and the best way for them to do that was for me to stop the game to allow them to express themselves.'"

And boy, did they ever.

The game paused as Davies left the field. He embraced each of his coaches, teammates, and even his parents, who had been escorted down to the sideline. His eyes twinkled as Victoria tried to cradle him like a baby. They both laughed as she failed to do so.

Since Davies *still* wasn't old enough to win Vancouver's man of the match award, the club instead awarded the honour to Debeah and Victoria.

After the game, Davies spent several minutes walking around the field, saying his goodbyes. He signed autographs. He posed for photos, including one with Vancouver Canucks legends Henrik and Daniel Sedin, who would often attend games with their kids. And with his arm around his little brother's shoulder, he walked through the tunnel and disappeared into the bowels of BC Place for the final time of his Whitecaps career. Once he got to the locker room, he was presented with the official game ball to a chorus of cheers from his teammates.

"You guys pushed me to my limits," he told them. "Thank you guys so much."

It was a storybook ending — an "I was there" moment.

And one that will forever live in the folklore of the club and city.

"How often do you see a 17-year-old get a send-off like that?" Kamara said. "It was perfect. Being at home, the message was always 'This is your house. Entertain everybody in this house. All the kids in here are like, Phonzie, Phonzie! They're not screaming Kei. I score more goals than you, but they don't really care. It's you.'"

"All of Vancouver accepted Alphonso as their own," Teibert said. "When they were watching, it was like they were watching their son play. If he made a mistake, they would cheer him on. If he did something great, they would cheer him on. You just wanted him to get the ball. Every time he got the ball from when he was 15 years old to the time he left, it was just like this buzz of electricity that something was going to happen. Everyone took pride in watching him play."

A swarm of reporters awaited Davies in the press conference room after he left the field. He took to his seat in front of the bright lights with a little wave and his goofy grin.

"Testing, one two," he said as he tapped on the mic twice.

One of the reporters asked him if before going to bed the previous night he pictured waking up and scoring in his Whitecaps finale the following day.

"No, no, I was actually watching *Fortnite* before I went to sleep, so that was running through my mind," Davies laughed, once again showing off his braces and beloved smile.

It was another reminder that he was still a kid.

A kid ready to conquer the world.

CHAPTER 9:
MIA SAN MIA (PART I)

"Sorry, sorry, sorry," Davies said, with a Canadian flag wrapped around his waist.

It couldn't have been any more Canadian. And yet this was a place no Canadian men's national team player had ever been before.

On August 23, 2020, Davies etched his name into the history books by winning the UEFA Champions League with Bayern Munich, the exclamation point to a sensational season that saw him emerge as a household name in Europe and one of the world's very best players at his position.

Davies, 19, was the youngest player on the pitch. That was nothing new. His youthfulness belied his composure on the day. On the grandest of stages, Davies played the full 90 minutes in a 1–0 win over PSG, the same team that had tried to pry him from Bayern's grasp a few years prior.

Neymar broke down in tears as he sat next to Kylian Mbappé in the dugout. PSG's two-headed half-a-billion-dollar monster had been slain. They both covered their eyes as celebrations began.

A stage was assembled at the centre of the field. Medals were awarded. And amid a sea of flying confetti, Davies and his teammates lifted the European Cup. As suggested by Queen's iconic anthem ringing through the speakers, they were, in fact, the champions.

"It's everything you dream of as a kid," Davies told BT Sport following the match, donning a medal around his neck and a red Champions of Europe T-shirt that blended with the Maple Leaf around his waist. "Growing up in Edmonton, cold Edmonton, coming to Europe and winning the Champions League with a great club like Bayern is just everything you can ask for."

"Look out!" the reporter shouted moments later, as two of Davies's teammates appeared from off-camera and emptied a couple of water bottles over his head.

Naturally, Davies's first concern was the status of his phone, because what would a championship celebration in the 21st century be without a cellphone? He quickly placed it down as he barked at his teammates who were fleeing the scene. He put his hat back on — backwards, of course, with a little tilt to the side. He wiped down his face. And as only a Canadian would, he apologized repeatedly for the interruption.

"I want to inspire people with my story," Davies continued when asked about his improbable journey from a refugee camp. "It just goes to show that you can do anything you set your mind to."

Like winning the most coveted prize in club football.

This was Bayern's sixth European title, which put them third in the all-time rankings behind Real Madrid and AC Milan. Their first three titles came consecutively in the 1970s, thanks in part to the legendary Franz Beckenbauer and Gerd Müller. And their next three were spread out following the turn of the century, in 2001, 2013, and 2020.

Winning is a part of their DNA.

At Bayern Munich, there's no room for error. Every pass matters. Every training session. Every touch. Conceding a goal can cause alarm bells, let alone losing a game or, worse, a championship. Consider this: after a disappointing exit from the Champions League in 2022, Bayern head coach Julian Nagelsmann revealed that he received 450 death threats. Earlier that season, star Bayern winger Leroy Sané was booed by some of the club's own fans.

In addition to competing for continental glory, Bayern is expected to win the Bundesliga and the DFB-Pokal, Germany's top league and domestic cup competition, every single year.

And they usually do.

They're the German "Rekordmeister," having won a whopping 31 Bundesliga championships as of the year 2022, compared to just five by the next closest teams. And they're the pride and joy of the region.

Not anyone can play at Bayern Munich.

It's not enough to have potential, or to be talented.

"You must be extraordinarily talented," Michael Reschke said.

Reschke saw this first-hand during his three years as Bayern's technical director.

One of his first signings was Joshua Kimmich, who blossomed into a linchpin for both Bayern and the German national team. At the time, though, he'd only played in Germany's second and third divisions.

"I had a long, strong conversation with [then-Bayern Munich CEO] Karl-Heinz Rummenigge because we paid a 9.5-million-euro transfer fee for Joshua Kimmich," Reschke said. "And Rummenigge told me, 'He's 18 years old, he hasn't played one minute in the Bundesliga. How can we spend so much?'"

At big clubs like Bayern, it's not always an easy ride for young players. When winning is everything, it can go one of two ways. It can help a young player raise their level. Or it can have the opposite effect and come at the expense of their development.

"In the mind of Manuel Neuer, Robert Lewandowski, or Thomas Müller, it's not to support young kids just to support them," Reschke said of the three Bayern legends. "Yes, they will support him, but only if he's at the level and they know he can help us to win. They don't want to develop. They want to win. You have to respect this mentality, and you have to feel it inside yourself, to be a successful Bayern Munich player."

These are the reasons Davies's transfer to Bayern was met with a fair amount of skepticism. Many suggested that he should have instead moved to a mid-level European team, where he'd be able to get more playing time to develop his game and showcase his abilities.

He wasn't ready for a big club like Bayern, they said.

"After we signed, everybody was calling me, agents that I knew, they were saying you made the biggest mistake, you're going to ruin this kid's life," Huoseh recalled. "He's going to go to Bayern and sit on the bench, they're going to move him to their second team, maybe loan him out. He's just going to get lost."

There's no way a teenager from Canada would be able to make it at Bayern, right?

Wrong.

"He was not a 17- or 18-year-old Canadian boy," Reschke said. "He was Alphonso Davies."

Marco Neppe stood next to Davies and his parents as they said goodbye at the Edmonton International Airport. The papers had been signed. Davies's future had been decided.

And it was time to go.

"Be a good guy," Davies's mom reminded him.

It's a moment that lives long in Neppe's memory. A reminder that this was more than a sporting transaction. Rather, the life of this young man was now in their hands.

"We will take care of him," they assured her.

"For us, at the moment, it felt like, hey, this is now our responsibility," Neppe recalled. "For sure, he has to perform and football is all about performing and working — having fun in our club and enjoying, that's quite important as well. But for us, we put him out to a different culture, to a different country, far far away from parents and his friends, so we understood directly; this is now our job. We have to take care of him. He's a young guy. And he should never lose his smile. We worked hard and invested a lot of energy that he would never lose his smile. That was our job now."

Davies moved to Munich in November 2018, a few weeks after his 18th birthday. He was greeted at the airport with a Bayern jacket, jersey, and scarf. The jersey was crested with his name and new number, 19 — the age he'd be turning in 2019, his first season with the club.

"Mia san family," translated as "We are family," was written on the scarf overtop of Canada's Maple Leaf and America's stars and stripes. Bayern has a strong North American brand. And their motto, "Mia san Mia," or "We are who we are," resonates deeply amongst their players, staff, and supporters alike.

Bayern has 16 "golden rules" that define Mia san Mia. Some of the principles listed include tradition, self-belief, diversity, and respect. Thomas Müller once described Mia san Mia as the "complete will to succeed," according to the official Bundesliga website. When Franck Ribéry bid a tearful goodbye to the Bayern supporters at the end of 2019, "Mia san Mia" were his final words. Ultimately, the phrase means something a little different to everyone. But there's one overarching theme.

"Most importantly, we are one family," the final principle states.

This is something Bayern prides itself on. Three-quarters of the club, in fact, is owned by fans. And some of the highest-level executives are alumni. There really is a family feel about it.

Now Davies was part of the family too.

The club helped him find an apartment, provided a vehicle as part of their partnership with Audi, and set him up with German lessons. On his first night in Munich, Davies watched Bayern's basketball team play at the Audi Dome. There, he casually played some one-on-one with his new teammate Serge Gnabry.

The next day, he traded the hardwood for the grass fields of Säbener Street, where he trained with the team for the first time. That's when things got real. The first player he saw in the locker room was a living legend. One of the most famous Dutch players of all time.

The man himself, Arjen Robben.

Robben's resumé included league titles in the Netherlands, England, Spain, and several in Germany. He scored the winning goal in a UEFA Champions League Final. He played in three Euros and three World Cups, leading the Oranje to a second-place finish in 2010 and a third-place finish in 2014.

He was also the same player Davies's junior-high coach compared him to as a Grade 7 student. And the same player Davies, a fellow left-footed winger, was being touted by some to ultimately replace.

"I couldn't believe what my eyes were seeing," Davies told BBC's *Football Focus* of his first encounter with Robben. "He came up to me, shook my hand, and said, 'How are you doing? I'm Arjen.'"

"You don't really need to introduce yourself," Davies thought.

The "Jedi Master and his Padawan," as Bayern's official North American Twitter account called the duo, walked shoulder to shoulder as they emerged from the locker room. Call it destiny or call it dumb luck, it was a fitting beginning to Davies's overseas adventure.

Also fitting: it was cold. Not quite Edmonton cold. But still below-freezing cold. The weather, in fact, was the topic of their conversation as Davies and Robben stepped onto the training pitch.

Shortly later, the coach called the players in for a huddle. A large circle formed, and Davies was introduced to a round of applause. One of his new teammates, Sandro Wagner, grabbed Davies's left arm, lifted it up in the air, and gently patted him on the back.

Mia san Mia.

Despite the warm welcome, it took Davies some time to adjust to his new surroundings. For the first time in his life, he was truly on his own. In Vancouver, he lived with a billet family and went to school.

Now it was just him, alone, on the other side of the world.

"After training, he'd just go home," said Chernoh Fahnbulleh, an old friend from Edmonton who came to visit a couple of times. "He didn't really know what else to do."

He didn't know the city. He didn't know the language. And although he got along with his new teammates right away, he didn't really have any real friends on the team.

Until he met Chris Richards and Joshua Zirkzee, a pair of up-and-coming talents who had also recently joined Bayern from abroad. All three of them were around the same age. And all three of them spoke English. So they naturally gravitated towards each other.

"It was kind of like our group," Zirkzee said.

At first, Zirkzee was a bit hesitant to approach Davies. The Dutchman had been playing for Bayern's youth teams. He was one year younger than Davies. And he had seen videos of him on 433, one of the most popular soccer accounts on social media, "just smashing everyone in the U.S.

"For me, it was like, 'This guy's a big deal,'" Zirkzee recalled.

But Zirkzee knew how hard it could be for someone who doesn't speak German to come into the club and city. So he started talking to Davies, and they hit it off instantly.

"When I first spoke to him and noticed this guy is very down to earth, you just had to respect that," Zirkzee said, referencing their early conversations at Bayern's January 2019 training camp in Qatar.

Unlike Davies, who lived by himself, Zirkzee and Richards lived at the FC Bayern Campus with other players from the club's youth set-up. In addition to a residence, the campus had a Mensa, or cafeteria, where three meals were provided per day. It also had a beach volleyball court and rock-climbing wall for leisurely activities. And, of course, it had the training fields for all the youth teams.

So they never really had to leave.

"We were kind of confined to this complex," said Richards, who had been playing for Bayern's U-19s.

It wasn't until Davies arrived that they started venturing out into the city. Together, the three of them spent a lot of time exploring Munich. They liked shopping — though they were surprised to learn that almost everything was closed on Sundays — and going out to eat. And when they weren't roaming around town, they usually set up shop at Davies's apartment to hang out and play video games.

"Wherever we went, we always just seemed to have a lot of fun," Richards said.

Richards and Davies had more in common than most players at Bayern Munich.

A native of Birmingham, Alabama, Richards also came through an MLS academy, with FC Dallas. He and Davies actually played against each other at the annual U.S. Soccer Development Academy Winter Showcase in December 2017, the year before they both moved to Munich.

They weren't just two young players trying to make it. They were two young North Americans trying to make it.

That felt different.

"I think it kind of gives you an extra chip on your shoulder, because a lot of these guys are European," Richards said. "I think most coaches, even if it's in the U.S. or if it's here, are more likely to give a European guy a chance because they're kind of just perceived as better football players than us . . . It's kind of like you go from being the man in your MLS academy, then you end up coming here and you're like the bottom of the totem pole."

Richards and Davies knew they had something to prove. And before getting into a game, they knew they'd have to do it on the training field. At Bayern, that was easier said than done.

"They expect perfection," Richards said.

That's something he learned very quickly. In one of his very first training sessions, Richards played a pass to Robben's right foot instead of his favoured left.

And he heard about it.

"He looked at me crazy and kind of cursed me out," Richards recalled.

The veteran players on the team have very high standards. And when those standards aren't met, "they'll let you know," Zirkzee said, adding that Müller and Kimmich were the most vocal in training.

Right away, Davies realized that the quality at Bayern was on another level.

A world-class level.

"The passing, their touches, their control, everything is just so on point," he told *ESPN FC*. "You have about two seconds to make a decision after you get the ball, so you really have to know what you're going to do with the ball or where your first pass is going to be, or your next dribble. You have to really look around. I think that's where I struggled at first."

Then there were the rondos. Those pesky rondos.

A rondo is a common warmup exercise, similar to keep-away, in which a group of players form a circle around another player or two and try to pass the ball around them. It can get extremely competitive. And it can get extremely loud, especially if someone pulls off a nutmeg, passing the ball through the legs of the player in the middle.

Just ask Davies.

"I think the first time I was in the middle, I got 'megged by Jérôme [Boateng] twice," Davies laughed as he recounted the story to BBC. "It was a big comedy show."

After his first week of training, one German tabloid newspaper reported that Davies's performance was "no reason to be euphoric."

113

They doubled down a few months later, stating in a headline that "Davies is not good enough for Bayern yet."

It was a premature assessment, but it also spoke to the challenge that was ahead of him and the increased scrutiny he'd be facing.

From day one, the pressure was on.

Davies got his first minutes for Bayern Munich on January 13, 2019, against fellow Bundesliga side Borussia Mönchengladbach. It wasn't an official league outing but a 45-minute game in the final of the Telekom Cup, a single-day tournament featuring four German teams.

With Robben injured, Davies started on the right wing next to Colombian attacking midfielder James Rodríguez. Naturally, he looked a bit tentative at first. But in the 20th minute, he caught the eye with a clever back-heel touch through the legs of the opposing defender. Then in the 45th minute, he nearly drew a penalty by beating the same defender, this time using his speed to round the corner before getting clipped in the box.

Bayern won the game in a penalty shootout. Neuer, the team captain, instructed Davies to lead the ensuing celebration. His smile radiated as he hoisted the trophy.

It would be his first of many.

But it wasn't all smooth sailing from there.

In some ways, Davies's time in Munich started the same way as his time in Vancouver. He was in and out of the lineup, he spent some time with the second team, and there were some learning lessons — like the time he was reportedly issued a hefty fine for being late to training due to airport delays upon his return from France, where he was visiting then-girlfriend and fellow budding soccer star Jordyn Huitema.

But just like in Vancouver, Davies showed flashes of brilliance right away.

One of the highlights from his first season came on March 17, 2019, at the Allianz Arena, a futuristic 75,000-seat stadium that rests majestically upon the northern tip of Munich. At night, the plastic panels of its exterior — illuminated in Bayern red on gamedays

— provide a glow that lights up the sky and can be seen from the neighbouring Austrian mountaintops.

Some have described it as a landmark. Others a crown jewel. To Munich, it's a "football temple." And on that rainy Sunday night, Davies got his baptism.

He entered the game as a substitute in the 59th minute with Bayern leading 5–0. It was only his fifth league appearance. The previous ones were even shorter cameos, playing 4 minutes, 13 minutes, 1 minute, and 7 minutes, respectively. This time, he had half an hour to make an impact.

That he did.

In the 70th minute, a rebound fell to him at the centre of the box. Before the ball could hit the ground, Davies struck it out of mid-air with the inside of his weaker right foot to score his first goal in the Bundesliga. With his arms extended from side to side like an airplane and the rain falling onto his smiling face, Davies ran to the corner flag and slid to his knees — having recently watched some videos of Robben celebrating the same way on that very field.

As it turns out, Davies stretched a knee ligament during his celebration. But in that moment, it felt like he was on top of the world. The first player to join him in celebration was Ribéry, a Bayern icon and the other half of Robbery, which made for another fitting picture.

At 18 years, four months, and 15 days old, Davies became Bayern's youngest goalscorer in nearly 20 years.

"Alphonso's a real diamond," Bayern sporting director Hasan Salihamidžić said after the match, as quoted on the Bundesliga website. "He's the future for sure, but he has also shown he has a role to play in the here and now."

Still, Davies found it difficult to get consistent playing time. Early the following season, with Robben and Ribéry departed, he even spoke with his agent about the potential of a loan.

"Listen, if that's what you really want, I can definitely work on it," Huoseh remembered telling him. "There are definitely clubs that will take you out on loan. But let's see what happens here. Be patient."

Huoseh had known Davies for a long time. About a decade. He usually had a good sense of how Davies was feeling. And on that phone call, he sensed something different.

"That's the one time where I really felt like, oh jeez, Alphonso was kind of down, you know?"

That fall, Huoseh made a trip to Munich with his wife and Davies's mom. Davies was moving into a new place, so they figured it was a good time to visit and help with the move.

It was also around this time that two of Bayern's starting defenders, Lucas Hernández and Niklas Süle, went down with injuries. Hernández, who had just won the World Cup with France, was Bayern's big-money signing. They paid a club and league record fee of around US$90 million to acquire the defender, significantly more than what they paid for Davies.

Prior to his injury, Hernández was playing as a left-sided defender, or a left back. Davies, who is known for his attacking abilities, had played some left back previously both in Vancouver and in a couple of his early appearances with Bayern.

So Niko Kovač, Bayern's head coach at the time, decided to throw him in. Davies got his first Bundesliga start on October 26, 2019 — a 2–1 win over FC Union Berlin.

"Maybe his mom was a good luck charm," Huoseh said. "I don't know, but we got to Germany and he ended up playing in those two matches that we watched."

Then he played the next one. And the next one. And the one after that.

"We wanted to give him all the trust that it's not random that he's here, or it's a one-time chance and if you grab it, it's good, and if not, you have to go," Neppe said. "We wanted to give him the feeling that 'Hey, this is your new home. We trust in you. We believe in you. Do what you love.'"

Davies started a whopping 30 straight matches that season. Even after Hernández returned to full health. Even after Kovač was replaced by Hansi Flick as head coach. And not only in the Bundesliga but also the German Cup and, of course, the Champions League.

This was his spot now.

"I told him, 'Phonzie, you got the opportunity, you now have this position, make it difficult for anybody to take it away from you. This is yours, you have to work even harder to keep it,'" Huoseh recalled. "He was really happy. He goes to me, 'I don't care where they put me on the field. I just want to play.' And hey, he turned out to be one of the best left backs in the world."

There wasn't a singular performance that put Davies into that category. It was a body of work throughout the season, and it would be unfair to suggest otherwise. But his star showing against Chelsea in the Champions League Round of 16 served as a coming-out party.

"I remember telling him, 'You better enjoy that Champions League anthem because I have a feeling tonight's going to be crazy,'" Zirkzee recalled of a conversation he had with Davies when they walked into the stadium. "In the second half, because he played on the side where the bench was, the only thing I saw was just *whoosh whoosh*, up and down. Alphonso was just too quick."

"Before that game, he was already doing it," Zirkzee continued. "But now that he did it in a Champions League game, of course, it gets different recognition. I think we all had that vibe like, 'Yeah, man, you deserve it.'"

February 25, 2020.

That was the day Davies announced himself to the world. The day Bayern's supporters chanted his name at Stamford Bridge. The day he was trending worldwide on Twitter.

As it turns out, it was also the day that Huoseh and Salihamidžić laid the groundwork for a new contract that would net Davies a healthy raise and extend his stay at the club an additional two years, until 2025.

Huoseh was in the stands that Tuesday night in London. He sat alongside Bayern's travelling fans at the south end of the stadium and had a front-row seat to Davies's unworldly assist to Lewandowski.

Following the match, Salihamidžić pulled Huoseh aside at a team gala.

"Let's talk. We need to do a deal," Huoseh remembered him saying amongst the sound of joyful chattering and music in the background.

It wasn't the first time Salihamidžić had raised the topic.

They'd met in Germany a month prior but couldn't agree on the terms. Huoseh wasn't in any rush. This was Davies's first full season with the team — he'd joined midway through the previous one. He still had three more years left on his contract.

"Isn't it early?" Huoseh remembered asking.

"They said, 'No, we want to reward him because of the way he's playing.' They knew. They knew they had something special."

The conversation continued in Salihamidžić's hotel room after the gala. Negotiations went late into the night. But Huoseh said they were still "a little bit off." And he had a flight back to Canada early the next morning, so he left just after midnight.

"Just leave it," Huoseh said. "You've got him for another three years, so don't worry about it."

About an hour later, Huoseh's phone pinged.

It was Salihamidžić.

"Can you come to Germany?" the message read.

After some back and forth, Huoseh reluctantly obliged. And he's glad he did. The next day, after another round of negotiations, Davies put pen to paper on a new deal that is believed to have bumped his annual salary to the neighbourhood of US$6 to $8 million.

"We were going to hold out," Huoseh said. "And Alphonso was encouraged by certain entities to hold out, but it would have been the biggest mistake we made."

That's because just a few weeks later, the financial landscape changed.

Everything did.

CHAPTER 10:
MIA SAN MIA (PART II)

On March 11, 2020, the World Health Organization declared COVID-19 a global pandemic — defined, in simplest terms, as the "worldwide spread of a new disease." Caused by a new strain of the coronavirus, COVID-19 had already infected more than 118,000 people in 114 different countries at that point. There were more than 4,000 deaths.

As feared, it was very much just the beginning.

That same day, the NBA announced that it was suspending its season after a player tested positive for the virus. Two days later, the Bundesliga did the same. In the blink of an eye, sports came to a halt.

And so did the rest of the world.

Businesses were shut down. Borders were closed. Masks were mandated — when Davies's contract extension was finally announced to the public, he and Bayern's executives wore white face coverings as they posed for photos in a spaced-out boardroom.

Living in isolation, or small bubbles, and physical distancing from others became the norm. Many lives were lost.

Millions.

It was also a period of social unrest, triggered by the murder of George Floyd, a Black man, by a white police officer in Minneapolis. Protests for racial justice, in support of the Black Lives Matter movement, were held all over the world.

Sports seemed trivial.

But for some, they helped provide a little light in a time of darkness.

Following a two-month hiatus and a seven-day quarantine training camp, the Bundesliga became the first major sports league to return amidst the ongoing pandemic.

It certainly wasn't a return to normalcy. A rigorous safety protocol was implemented in collaboration with local governments and medical experts. Matches would be played behind closed doors, without spectators. Players and staff would be tested regularly, travel to stadiums in multiple buses, and use multiple locker rooms to avoid congestion in small spaces. Coaches and other staffers would be required to wear masks and practise physical distancing.

It looked a little different, but it was a framework that would soon be emulated in various leagues around the sporting world. For now, though, all eyes were on Germany.

With all the other major sports leagues still suspended, the Bundesliga was under a greater microscope. Record TV ratings were reported.

And Davies delivered.

In Bayern's second game back from the break, he had a goal and an assist against Eintracht Frankfurt. The game after that, he drew praise for helping Bayern keep a clean sheet in a top-of-the-table clash against Borussia Dortmund. And the game after that, he scored again, somehow dribbling through four Fortuna Düsseldorf defenders that had him surrounded — not unlike some of the goals he scored in MLS. He picked up right where he left off in the game against Chelsea. But he saved his best moment for an even bigger stage.

It was August 14, 2020. The UEFA Champions League quarterfinal. Bayern Munich vs. Barcelona. The first time Davies would face Lionel Messi, his childhood idol.

As it came in the midst of the pandemic, the game would be played without spectators. Huoseh, therefore, watched from back in Edmonton.

"I remember telling my son Adam, 'I hope Alphonso doesn't freeze up when he sees Messi,'" Huoseh recalled. "Starts blushing, turns red . . . I thought he would be nervous."

Davies would later tell reporters that his heart was "beating faster and faster" every time Messi got the ball on his side of the field. But no one would have been able to tell.

Bayern won the game 8–2. No, that's not a typo.

And Davies was trending again on that day after serving up "one of the finest assists in living memory," as described by the official website of the Bundesliga.

Fittingly, the play started along the left touchline with Davies picking up a loose ball and rounding Messi, the first Barcelona player to approach him. Next, he skipped past Arturo Vidal, causing the Chilean national team midfielder to lose his footing and slam the pitch in disgust.

This is where it got really fun.

After breaking the ankles of Vidal, as the kids say, Davies continued running down the left wing. Eventually, he stopped on a dime a few yards before the corner flag, resulting in a one-v-one with Portuguese right back Nélson Semedo.

There wasn't a ton of space. Semedo was right in his grill.

Not for long.

"Let me try something," Davies thought in that moment, as he recounted in the Amazon Prime documentary *FC Bayern — Behind the Legend.*

With a little shimmy and shoulder drop, Davies blew by the defender as he toed the endline and approached the goal. There were four other Bayern players in the box. Serge Gnabry was open near the top of the area. Robert Lewandowski was at the front post. Ivan Perišić was at the back post. They were all decent options.

Davies chose the best one, instead finding the late runner and putting the ball on a platter for Joshua Kimmich, who simply tapped it into the open net.

"Unbelievable," Kimmich said after the match. "I was almost ashamed of how happy I was after scoring, because it was obviously 99 percent his goal."

"You bring joy to my eyes when I see u play kid!" Marcelo commented on Instagram, high praise from one of the best left backs to ever play the game.

It was arguably the best highlight of his career to date. But it may not have even been the highlight of his day. That came a bit earlier.

There was a moment in the first half where Messi clipped the back of Davies's heels as the Canadian broke away down the left. Davies fell to the pitch. The referee called a foul.

What happened next was what made it special.

Messi offered his hand and helped pull Davies up from the ground.

"Here's a kid looking up to his idol, playing against his idol, and his idol's fouled him and helping him up," Davies told reporters. "It's everything you could ask for as a footballer."

Naturally, the moment was caught on camera. DAZN, the Canadian rights holder for UEFA Champions League matches, subsequently tweeted the photo with a caption that read: "The best player in the world . . . getting helped up by Lionel Messi" and a wink-face emoji.

"I sent him the picture," Huoseh said. "I was like, 'Did your face turn red? Were you shaking when he came to pick you up?' He goes, 'Nah, it was good.' We were just joking about it. You think he's going to get super nervous, but he kept his composure. He knows when he's out there, he's there to do a job."

But that doesn't mean he didn't want a little keepsake.

Leading up to that day, Davies sent Messi a direct message on Instagram asking to swap jerseys after the match — a common tradition in soccer.

"I'm number 19, the left back," he wrote, as confirmed by a member of his agency.

The message was never read.

So during the game, when the score was tied in the first half, he asked in person.

Messi agreed.

When the game was over, they spoke again and planned to meet in the tunnel. Davies was there first. But then he was pulled into a room for a random doping test. He asked some of his teammates if they'd go and get the jersey for him.

No one wanted to — after losing 8–2, they figured Messi wouldn't be in the best mood.

"By the time I was out of [the doping test], he was already on the bus," Davies said. "So I wasn't trying to go on the bus and bother him."

He didn't get the jersey, but he did get his keepsake. The framed photo of Messi offering his hand is now up on the wall in the basement of his Edmonton home.

"Me going up against him was just a dream come true," Davies said.

Davies's success came during a historic season for Bayern, who won 29 of their final 30 matches to complete the "sextuple" — a clean sweep of all six trophies available to them. They were only the second team to ever accomplish the feat, joining Barcelona's famous 2009 squad. They were also the first team to win each of their matches in the UEFA Champions League.

It was an utterly dominant campaign. And a 19-year-old Canadian featured prominently, playing the sixth most minutes out of any of the team's outfield players, scoring three goals, and recording eight assists from his defensive position.

"It was crazy because we all knew he had the talent, but it was just a matter of when he'd be able to show that," Chris Richards said. "He got on the field, it was like assist, goal, assist, assist, assist, every game. Or he'd do some type of crazy action and everyone was like, 'Ah shit, Phonzie just did that.' It wasn't just us noticing. Clearly, the whole world noticed."

The accolades quickly started piling up.

Bundesliga Rookie of the Year.

Canadian Men's Soccer Player of the Year.

UEFA Champions League Squad of the Season.

FIFA FIFPRO World 11, the first North American to join the likes of Messi and Cristiano Ronaldo on the prestigious list of the world's best 11 players in a given season.

He was also a co-winner of the Northern Star Award (formerly the Lou Marsh Trophy), awarded to the top athlete in Canada, becoming the first male soccer player to ever earn the honour.

Part of what made Davies's 2020 season especially notable was the fact that only once before had a Canadian-born men's player hoisted the UEFA Champions League trophy. That was Owen Hargreaves, a fellow Albertan, who won it once with Bayern and once with Manchester United in the early 2000s.

But there was a caveat.

Hargreaves opted to represent England, the birth country of his father, rather than Canada on the international stage. His decision didn't sit well with the Canadian soccer community, to put it lightly.

Davies, on the other hand, was wearing the Canadian flag with pride.

Literally.

He wore it late into the night on August 23, 2020, as Bayern held a celebratory banquet following their Champions League triumph. The flag now draped around his neck, hanging behind him, Davies went live on Instagram to enjoy the moment with his fans and friends.

"Then something just clicked in my head," he told reporters a few weeks later.

He decided to ask for an Instagram follow from Drake, a famous rapper and fellow Canadian. Just minutes later, Drake obliged. And with a reimagination of "Informer" – one of the biggest hits to ever come out of Canada — blaring in the background, Davies simply "lost it."

"Drizzy! Oh my god!" he screamed. "Drake! You followed ME?

"My night is complete!" he continued. "I'm going to bed, I'm going to bed!"

Shortly later, Davies received a message from Drake that read "Congrats King."

He was a king of Europe. And a king of the north too.

CHAPTER 11:
ROAD RUNNER

"Meep meep."
It's the Road Runner.

The fleet-footed bird kicks up a cloud of dust and escapes the scene. His long and skinny legs are moving so fast they become a blur.

Catch him if you can.

Wile E. Coyote tries his very best to. He tries every trick in the book.

But the Road Runner is always one step ahead.

See where this is going? If not, Thomas Müller will take care of the rest.

"The opponent thinks, 'Oh, I have time, I have time,' and then 'Meep meep, meep meep,' the Road Runner, the FC Bayern Road Runner, comes ahead and steals the ball," the decorated Bayern Munich midfielder said when describing Davies in 2020.

It was an impressive impersonation of the Looney Tunes character. Like, spot-on.

And it was an apt description of Davies.

He got his new nickname following a resolute defensive performance in the German Clásico, an always-anticipated matchup between Bayern and Borussia Dortmund, one of their biggest challengers in the Bundesliga. In any given season, this is a game German soccer supporters have circled on their calendars. And this was just the third week back from the COVID shutdown, which only added to the intrigue.

In the 33rd minute, Dortmund phenom Erling Haaland poked the ball around Bayern's last man back and appeared to be in on goal for an uncontested opportunity. As one of Europe's most prolific goalscorers, Haaland would have been licking his chops.

"Meep meep."

Trailing the play by 12.5 metres, Davies shifted into high gear and closed down Dortmund's prized striker in the span of just 3.1 seconds. It was like he was playing a video game and decided to hit the turbo button. This is why people call him a "cheat code."

Haaland never had a chance.

"Alphonso davies is fast as f***," longtime English Premier League and Belgian national team striker Romelu Lukaku tweeted moments later.

"Bro . . . he can FLY," NBA big man Larry Nance Jr. agreed.

Davies was clocked at 35.3 kilometres an hour on that sprint. And here's the thing: he was still picking up steam.

As the head of physical preparation at the Whitecaps, Jon Poli worked directly with Davies throughout his time in Vancouver. Poli and the sports science team would track all sorts of data. Every week, they did maximum velocity sprinting with the players in training. Davies just kept progressing as his body filled out. And he eventually hit 37.8 kilometres an hour, which was even faster than what was recorded in the Bundesliga.

"That would put him at the top of any league," Poli said.

It's also around the same speed that Usain Bolt averaged when he set a new world record for the 100-metre sprint in 2009, though his top speed in that race was 44.72 kilometres an hour.

Typically, players will be faster in training than they are in games. A controlled, unobstructed environment can be created in training. Not so much in games, where Poli said players might only reach 90 or 95 percent of their maximum speed.

Unless you're Davies.

"He hit a max, like what we had seen in training, in one game where he just had this long, kind of linear acceleration where he really opened up," Poli said. "It was rapid."

When Davies gets going, he's a defender's worst nightmare.

Just ask Alistair Johnston, who lined up directly opposite to him in one of Johnston's first training sessions with the Canadian national team. It was an 11-v-11 scrimmage. Davies received the ball about 20 yards inside his own half before playing it forward to Cyle Larin.

Then Johnston realized what was about to happen.

"It was going to be a give-and-go and it was going to be a track meet," he recalled. "So instantly I decided, OK, it's time, let's try to break some GPS records here, try to break the speed of sound barrier, because I'm going to need to keep up with him. So I was absolutely into top gear right away trying to sprint and I thought, 'I'm here, I'm ahead of him for sure.' I still see Cyle Larin, he's just got such a calmness in his eyes when he's playing it. I was like, 'Why is he still playing this ball? I'm ahead here.' He slipped it down the channel and I thought I had a good chance. Then all of a sudden, I didn't even hear it, that was the scariest part. It was more of like just air moving. I'm more of a powerful runner, you can hear me coming, I'm chugging along. This was not the case. This was an F1 vehicle flying by. It sounded like Lewis Hamilton driving by me. It was all of a sudden a *whoosh* of air. I realized I was going as hard as I could and he was probably in second or third gear and gliding effortlessly by me.

"You've watched him on TV, you know what he's about, you know that he's probably the fastest player in the game," Johnston added. "But until you actually get to see it first-hand, it really is hard to truly grasp."

Comparisons to other sports and leagues are not exactly scientific. There are too many variables. Different measurement systems and surfaces can skew the results. But here's one thing that's indisputable: if Davies isn't the fastest soccer player on the planet, he's not far off.

"There's being fast, and there's being Phonzie fast," said Chris Richards, who cited Davies as the hardest player he's ever had to defend.

"He comes at you full speed, you stand no chance," added Pa-Modou Kah, who played more than 400 professional games in seven different countries.

Speed alone doesn't make a soccer player, however.

At least not a good one.

It's a big part of the reason Davies was able to adapt to the professional level so quickly as he developed in other areas. And it's a big part of what makes him such an electrifying talent. But it would be a disservice to Davies not to recognize the other elite parts of his game, because they're abundant.

baller
n. an athlete who plays a sport that involves the use of a ball
adj. extremely good or impressive; excellent

For starters, there's that little round ball. You know, the thing you have to kick with your feet. From an early age, Davies was able to do things with the ball that others simply couldn't.

"The truth is, we get all kinds of athletes with exceptional athleticism," Marco Bossio said of his junior-high soccer program in Edmonton. "The thing that separated Alphonso from the rest was his technique on the ball that coincided with his athleticism. That was rare."

It was his shot — volleys, bicycle kicks, scissor kicks, and all.

It was his footwork — as the adage goes, he could dribble in a phone booth.

And, in particular, it was the way he could run with the ball.

"He can be at top speed and remain in full control," said Russell Teibert, who played with Davies in Vancouver and for the Canadian national team. "Even when he looks like he's out of control, he's still in control."

It's been suggested that some of the best players in the world are even faster when they have the ball at their feet. While it may appear that way, it's not usually the case, from Poli's observations. But when Davies finds space in open field, takes those longer strides, and pushes the ball ahead of him, Poli said "he'd be getting pretty close."

"He's still faster with the ball than a lot of guys without the ball," he added.

When watching Davies play, and his ability to control the ball at high speeds, Bossio is reminded of a fellow household name in Edmonton and hockey's most exciting player.

This is a Canadian story, after all.

"The biggest comparison for me is a Connor McDavid type of hockey player," Bossio said.

Much like McDavid does on the ice, Davies often appears like he's gliding around his opponents as he attacks the goal. His ability to beat defenders in one-v-one situations while maintaining possession of the ball, known as a successful dribble, is almost superhuman. He makes it look easy.

It certainly looked that way during his time in MLS.

"He was obviously in another world, just a complete other stratosphere, in his ability to beat guys off the dribble," said Matthew Doyle, the lead analyst for MLSsoccer.com. "It was the straightforward speed, but the change of pace, the first step, the hesitation. Watch the way he uses his hips to set up defenders, just eliminating multiple defenders at a time. There haven't been a lot of guys like that in MLS at any age. There might have been zero guys like that in MLS at any age."

The numbers back up that claim.

Davies averaged 4.05 successful dribbles per 90 minutes during his time in MLS, according to Opta Sports. It was the highest clip of any MLS player who had at least 1,000 minutes under their belt between 2009, the earliest year in which there is data available, and Davies's final season in 2018.

He also completed the second-most dribbles in the Bundesliga in two of his first three full seasons at Bayern, according to Fbref. And it's not just the fact that Davies can get around defenders.

It's how he does it.

"It's not only speed, it's quick feet," said Marco Neppe, Bayern's chief-scout-turned-technical director.

A lot of times, it's Davies's fancy footwork that allows him to wriggle out of tight spaces and puts him into positions where he can use his speed. Davies plays with flair. He's not afraid to try things. The types of things kids like to try with their friends on the playground. The types of things that bring people out of their seats — pirouettes, stepovers, backheels, nutmegs.

And more often than not, he'll pull them off.

Case in point: Davies led the Bundesliga with 12 nutmegs in that first full season at Bayern, according to Fbref. That was also the second-highest total in Europe's top five leagues, just one back of Manchester United forward Marcus Rashford.

He can be in two-, three-, or four-man coverage with seemingly no way out.

He always finds a way out.

However, the end product wasn't there during the early stages of Davies's professional career. He would get around defenders with ease. And he would drag the team forward by carrying the ball towards the opponent's goal and away from his own, a highly valued component of the game known as a progressive carry.

But it wouldn't lead to much.

"I always gave him stick," Kah said. "I thought he didn't score enough."

Sometimes, he would make the wrong decision in the final third of the field. Other times, he would send his shots or crosses awry. Nevertheless, the Manchester United scout who was watching Davies closely still saw someone who was playing with a real "purpose."

The rest could come later.

"He may not finish the way he wants to, but he was running with a purpose of creating something dangerous, a cross, a shot to the goal, or creating a penalty," Jorge Alvial said.

"I thought this kid is not just speed. He's smart. He's football smart."

savvy
adj. having or showing a practical cleverness or judgment

One thing people don't always appreciate about the Road Runner?

He's always thinking.

In the cartoon, Wile E. Coyote devises all sorts of elaborate schemes to lure the Road Runner. He uses boulders, anvils, dynamite rockets, and the like. But the Road Runner is clever. He knows how to avoid the traps. Sometimes, he'll even bait the coyote before getting away.

Davies does the same when he's running at defenders.

As Doyle alluded to, he'll use his hips to disguise his movements. And he'll position the ball in a way that tempts defenders to lunge in. When they do, he'll fly right by them. Davies's highlight reel includes countless examples of him flicking the ball up in the air past sliding defenders, high enough that it loops over their bodies but low enough that he's able to maintain possession without breaking stride.

"If he wants you to be there, there's a reason for it," Johnston said, pointing again to his first attempt at defending Davies in training.

After playing the give-and-go with Larin, Johnston said, it seemed like Davies actually slowed down to let him catch up. And that's when he knew he was in trouble.

"He heel-chopped inside, and by the time I decelerated and turned around to look where he'd gone, he'd already played a give-and-go with Jonny David and was shooting on target," Johnston recalled. "It's one thing to be an unbelievable athlete in straight lines, but his ability to accelerate and decelerate, it was something I'd never seen before. And it was truly an eye-opening experience. Like, OK, that's what makes an elite, elite, world-class athlete."

Over time, opponents started to learn some of Davies's tendencies. They knew, for example, that he favoured his left foot and thrived on running along the outside. So defenders started to funnel him towards the middle of the field, where it's more congested.

But Davies found solutions.

"He doesn't have a weakness," said Canadian men's national team defender Kamal Miller. "Whatever you do, he's ready to do the opposite."

Nowadays, he'll often beat the first defender by coming inside. Or he'll play a quick one-two, or give-and-go, with one of his teammates — as he did against Johnston.

"What really made it all happen was when he was able to weaponize all that and turn it not just into these highlights, but into goals and assists in the box score," Doyle said.

That came in 2018. In that final MLS season, Davies looked like a man amongst boys.

Ironic, right?

Not only did the 17-year-old lead the league in successful dribbles, continuing to terrorize opposition defenders many years his senior, he also produced eight goals and 11 assists. And he created a league-high 10 goals as a direct result of a successful dribble, according to Fbref.

Like he did against Orlando in June 2018, a few days before his speech to FIFA Congress.

That was the game everything came together.

"He just blew up an entire team with his ability to get out into the open field," Doyle said. "But then once he was out in the open field, he wasn't just running fast at goal. He was manipulating them and their reactions as he manipulated the ball. He was sort of mapping the entire field."

One play in particular demonstrated those very qualities.

It started in Vancouver's own half, when Davies beat a sliding Orlando defender to a 50/50 ball a few yards before the halfway line. With the ball now at his feet, Davies opened his hips and changed his pace to freeze a second defender before dribbling around him with ease.

Now he had some space, but there was still work to do. As he ran down the left wing, Davies examined his options. He could try to dribble around another defender. He could shoot. Or he could try to pass to one of his two teammates who were already in the box.

He chose option four.

Davies faked a dribble to his left, turning the defender inside out, before threading a perfect pass to Kei Kamara, who was trailing the play and had found an opening in the box.

"He set up the entire defence, manipulated four or five professional defenders, to the point where all he had to do was slide the ball right into Kei's path for a one-touch finish," Doyle said. "That's elite. It's world-class. And he was doing that in MLS."

Before long, he'd be doing it in Europe too.

In fact, that very assist against Orlando felt a lot like the one he notched against Barcelona a few years later. If anyone wants to know what makes Davies special, all-time Whitecaps appearances leader Carl Valentine believes that's the play they should watch.

"That had his speed, his finesse, his awareness, his calm when he got in the box, it just had everything," said Valentine, a former winger who also played for the Canadian men's national team and at the highest level in England. "And it wasn't just a league game or training. It was the European quarterfinal. Like, wow."

The moment never seemed too big for Davies — whether it was the city championships with St. Nicholas, the Dallas Cup with Edmonton Strikers, his farewell game in Vancouver, or going up against his idol in the UEFA Champions League quarterfinal.

"He has no fear," Valentine said. "To him, it's like he's playing in his backyard."

In the eyes of John Herdman, a Vancouver-area resident who watched Davies closely during his time with the Whitecaps before coaching him with the Canadian national team, it's that quality that stands out above the rest. When the lights are shining, when the stakes are at their highest, Davies has an innate ability to rise to the occasion and truly express himself.

"That's what separates world-class from class," Herdman said.

determination
n. firm or unwavering adherence to one's purpose

Becoming a world-class talent doesn't just happen. It takes hard work. It takes determination. And that was never a problem for Davies.

With the Strikers, he had to run the stairs along Edmonton's river valley every weekend. There were about 300 steps. And Coach Nick had the team go up and down not once, not twice, but up to 20 times. Then they'd play a scrimmage.

"He wasn't always first," Huoseh said. "But most of the time he was."

At St. Nicholas, Bossio said Davies had "season's tickets" for the school's fitness room.

"I would preach to the kids, 'I'm not going to force you to go in there and work out. It has to be in you to want to be better,'" Bossio said. "Phonzie was one of those guys that was in there constantly, working on his leg strength, his endurance, his power."

He also set the school's record for the beep test, reaching level 14.4. Bossio has been having his athletes run that identical beep test for 15 years.

No one's come close to Davies's record.

"I tell the kids, 'The beep test measures your fitness levels, but it also measures your heart and your ability to push through pain,'"

Bossio said. "That was something Phonzie showcased to everybody. It showed this kid is fit, but he's also willing to do what others aren't."

Poli said Davies has an "incredible aerobic engine" that allows him to "run all day." A lot of times, an athlete will be fast but they won't be able to repeat high-intensity sprints without ample recovery time. Or they'll be extremely fit but won't be able to reach high speeds.

Davies has the best of both worlds. In junior high, for example, he won track and field city championships in both the 100-metre and 1,500-metre distances.

"It's a rare combination," Poli said. "It's the elite combination. And it's not just speed and endurance. His strength doesn't get talked about, but at 16 years old he was lifting heavier than some of our adult players. So he had a really good base of strength as well."

When Davies first started playing professionally, it was easy for him to get knocked off the ball. Nowadays, it's nearly impossible. In his final MLS season, for example, Davies led the league with 258 duels won, defined as a 50/50 contest between two opposing players.

He's become a sheer physical force.

It's easy to get caught up in calling Davies a naturally gifted athlete. While there may be some truth to such a statement, it doesn't account for the dedication he's always had towards mastering his craft — towards getting stronger, towards improving his right foot, towards understanding the tactical nuances of the game.

Davies was willing to work. He was willing to learn.

Talal Al-Awaid, one of his coaches at the Strikers, would be on the field with Davies up to six times a week during his youth soccer days. Davies was clearly more advanced than the rest of the group. So Al-Awaid and the coaches would look for different ways to challenge him.

"I recognize that every time you get the ball, you can take it and dribble past everybody and go score. But that's not going to help you at the next level," Al-Awaid would tell him. "Express yourself, dribble, have that creativity, but start recognizing when and where to do it."

Once or twice, Davies was even subbed out of the game to hammer home the point.

"Not as a punishment, just to have the conversation," Al-Awaid said. "At that next level, you're not just going to be able to dribble across your 18-yard-box in your defensive end. Having those conversations with him that typically you're not really having with too many players his age."

Davies was always receptive to feedback. There was never an argument. Never a frown.

And that would continue through the years.

In Vancouver, he'd often stay back at the end of training with Kamara and Kah, two of his mentors and older teammates. They'd work on all sorts of things: crosses, free kicks, one-v-one attacking and defending. There was a lot of information thrown at him.

And he was all ears.

"I saw this sponge that was willing to soak in whatever they told him, and he squeezes it when it's supposed to be squeezed," Kamara said. "Not many people can do that. He was somebody that didn't really know his ability, how good he is, but there was a light switch. Somebody would say, 'Hey, come on, you can do this,' and he did it exactly how you expected him to do it. That's a special talent there. Yes, people are talking about Phonzie's ability to run, his speed, this and that, but his understanding and the way he takes in information to me was the most important part."

Since they only spent one season together in Vancouver, Kamara joked that there's "no way" Davies should have listened to him. But he did. As a striker who feasted off crosses, Kamara encouraged Davies to send more balls into the box.

"My crosses are not that good," he remembered Davies saying.

"Nah, just cross it, and I'll try my hardest to be behind it," Kamara would tell him.

Once they started connecting, it only made Davies more dangerous. Get tight to him, he'll dribble around you. Give him space, he'll deliver a cross into the box.

Pick your poison.

This has translated to the next level. With Bayern, Davies is more of a provider than he is a goalscoring threat. He draws so much attention from opposing defenders that his teammates are often left wide open. And if someone else is in a better position to score, he'll almost always make the pass. With the Canadian men's national team, Davies tends to play with a greater desire to score goals, and even then, he was their all-time assist leader by age 21.

"I remember telling him, 'When you leave this country one day, you can run, run, run, but if your delivery is not sharp in the box, it doesn't mean anything,'" Kamara said. "But he was showing on the field at training that he wanted to learn, and I'm sure he's still doing that."

versatility
n. ability to adapt or be adapted to many different functions or activities

Davies had a lot to learn at Bayern. Mainly, how to play left back. He spent some time there in Vancouver, but it wasn't until the move to Bayern that it became his primary position.

In the modern game, left backs are still expected to join the attack and contribute offensively. They'll start from a deeper position on the field, which allows for more space to run into. This, of course, is Davies's bread and butter. Many of his assists at Bayern, in fact, have started with him winning a tackle in his own half before progressing the ball forward.

However, there are added responsibilities that come with being a defender. Not only is Davies still looking to create goals, now he needs to stop them too.

In his famous "Road Runner" interview, Müller pointed out how Davies can sometimes find himself in the wrong defensive position, forcing him to use his speed to recover. And that was something Davies acknowledged himself when asked about his new nickname.

"I'm happy to have the speed that I have," he said. "That's a factor in my game that I use very well. But I think over the years, going with this team, I think I'll definitely learn more about my position so it doesn't look like I'm out of position and just running back as fast as I can to catch up."

Davies's switch to left back was controversial, to say the least.

On the one hand, it helped him get regular minutes and play to some of his strengths. On the other, it limited his opportunities to truly unleash his attacking potential.

For that reason, former Whitecaps academy director Craig Dalrymple said he's sometimes left "wanting more" watching Davies play at Bayern.

"And that's not a criticism of him," Dalrymple said. "I just think there's so much more in the tank that he can provide in terms of excitement, flair, and creativity in the final third."

Neppe, for his part, said Davies plays "one of the most challenging positions on the pitch" at Bayern. Especially under new head coach Julian Nagelsmann, who demands tactical flexibility from his players and often has Davies playing further up the field as a wingback or even in more central attacking areas. And while his direct goal contributions are sometimes lacking, Davies consistently ranks among the 99th percentile of left backs in Europe's top five leagues at progressing the ball forward, as well as a host of other attacking categories.

"So if you're in this position, one of the best, or you want to be the best, this is great," Neppe said.

The idea of where to play Davies is something Herdman has thought long and hard about as the head coach of the Canadian men's national team. With Canada, Davies usually starts in attacking positions as their most dynamic offensive weapon. But he's been deployed all over the field — as a forward, a winger, a wingback, and a left back — depending on the game plan and opponent. Sometimes, he'll even be given the creative licence to roam around in a free role and end up playing multiple positions in the same game.

"What's great about Alphonso is he creates that dread in an opponent whether you play him higher or lower," Herdman told reporters in 2021. "When he's playing lower, he comes from those deep positions with space to run into. And then when he plays higher, he's such a threat in the transition when teams open up.

"It's a real conundrum at times," Herdman continued. "But at the same time, it's a gift that you've got somebody of his ability because of how his career has progressed. He's built that trajectory from being a carefree winger at the Vancouver Whitecaps to being a very disciplined left back at one of the best clubs in the world."

There was a learning curve at Bayern, to be expected. But very quickly, Davies made sure he could be relied upon. His athleticism certainly helped. As did the players that surrounded him, such as David Alaba, a natural left back who often played next to Davies in the centre back position. Another thing that helped?

His competitiveness.

"If you ever watch Phonzie when he loses the ball, and if the guy is still close to him, he'll grab onto the guy, he'll do whatever he can to win the ball back quickly," said Theo Bair, his former Whitecaps academy teammate. "It's not only his physical attributes and his skill, it's the mentality he has. He's relentless. He doesn't like losing the ball."

He takes it personally.

In the 2019–20 season, for example, Davies helped Bayern gain possession of the ball within five seconds of applying pressure on the opponent at the third-highest rate in the Bundesliga and the fifth-highest in Europe's top five leagues, according to Fbref.

This is exactly what Bair was referring to. It's a coach's dream. A lot of times, the number one thing they'll look at is how players react to losing the ball and the effort they put into the game when the other team has possession. It's not something everyone notices. But it's one of the first things Neppe did when he started scouting Davies.

"If he or a teammate loses the ball, he's really quick in his head to switch modes and fight to get the ball back," Neppe said. "It was like, hmm, wow."

Beyond the goals, assists, and dribbles, Davies does the little things that help his team win. Here's another one: in the 2020–21 season, he led the Bundesliga by tackling 66.7 percent of the dribblers that tried to take him on, according to Fbref.

Almost no one could get past him.

"There's almost nothing like watching this kid get on the ball and run at defenders and dribble," Doyle said. "But I hope that, as we all appreciate him, let's not let that completely overshadow the amount of work that he's obviously put in to learn to do the gritty, grimy, ugly things that defenders, even on Bayern Munich, have to do."

All these qualities, and many others, have helped turn Davies into one of the very best left backs in the world. It's more than just speed. It's more than the viral highlights. It's the "whole package," Neppe said. And he believes there's still more to come.

"I don't think that we can see the limit," Neppe added.

Davies has proven that he's not a "one-season wonder," as some suggested during the 2020–21 season, when he struggled with an injury. He just keeps getting better. And if his body can hold up to the rigours of professional soccer and the highly physical nature of his game, there's no reason to suggest he won't continue to do so.

"He will be one of the top three best players in the world, if he keeps growing the way that he's growing with his mentality," Alvial said. "I think he has the mentality that he's going to keep his feet on the ground, keep his head small, and continue to thrive. I believe he has that in him."

CHAPTER 12:
BORN ENTERTAINER

Theo Bair heard a knock on the door.

"I don't know anybody here," he thought. "What's going on?"

It was his first week in Vancouver. He had just moved from Ottawa to join the Whitecaps academy. His billet home hadn't been arranged yet, so he and a few other out-of-towners were staying in the dorm rooms at Fortius Sport & Health in Burnaby — now the Christine Sinclair Community Centre.

"I go and open my door, and there I see a young, bald, smiling Phonzie," Bair recalled.

"Hey man," he remembered Davies saying.

It was the first time they'd formally met. Davies, 14, had just joined the academy as well. Neither of them really knew anyone.

At least not yet.

"He just lets himself in, jumps on my bed, and starts talking to me," Bair said.

They've been good friends ever since.

Bair considers himself to be more of an introvert. But Davies has that type of infectious personality that rubs off on anyone in his presence. And that's exactly what happened.

"I think that he helped me a lot to express myself and be more of an outgoing person," Bair said.

Whenever Davies is around, things just happen. Whether you like it or not.

"He'll talk to people. He'll put his face in places. He'll dance. He'll sing. He'll do whatever," Bair said. "And not because he wants to put on a show, but just because that's him enjoying life."

That's Davies.

More than his soccer skills, it's that love for life that has touched the hearts of seemingly everyone who has been a part of his journey. Davies's unique mix of charisma and humility has helped him become a popular teammate and friend, a social media sensation whose hilarious TikTok videos have been seen by millions, and one of Canada's most beloved athletes.

"He's just a really good person," Russell Teibert said. "He has a really good heart."

That was there from the beginning.

The loud, goofy, outgoing Davies that sings Whitney Houston's "I Will Always Love You" in front of his Bayern teammates and hosts his own YouTube vlog?

Well, that took some time to develop.

Growing up, Davies was a quiet kid who liked to keep to himself, according to his parents. And those who first met him in Edmonton paint a similar picture.

"When I first met Alphonso, he didn't talk much," Huoseh said. "I'd crack a sarcastic joke and he'd kind of just look at me. I'd say, 'You know I'm just joking, right?' He'd be like, 'Ah, OK.'"

"I think he was quiet because you didn't know him," Gloire Amanda recalled of meeting Davies when he was in Grade 7. "His first year, I think he was the youngest in the whole squad. I think he was just more embarrassed than anything."

So what changed?

As refugees who come from similar backgrounds, Amanda and Davies both have the same answer.

It was the beautiful game.

"Football helped me make friends, football helped me express myself, football did a lot for me," Davies said in a roundtable discussion arranged by the UNHCR in 2021. "I was a shy guy in school, but once I started playing football, that's when I started making more and more friends.

"That's where I became myself."

After his first few games with the team, Amanda said, he rarely saw the shy side of Davies. But he pointed to one occasion where both extremes of his personality were on display.

Every year, Amanda and his family would attend an African cultural event in Edmonton where the community would gather at a big hall. One year, they brought Davies along. For the first hour, Amanda said, Davies was "extremely quiet" as they were eating dinner upstairs.

Then the music came on.

"Out of nowhere, he literally just left," Amanda said. "Me and my brothers were wondering where Alphonso went. So we went downstairs, and I found him literally on the dance floor."

There he was, dancing away with a bunch of strangers. The spotlights were shining. A couple of circles had formed. And everyone seemed to gravitate towards Davies.

Anyone who has spent enough time with Davies has a dancing story, it seems.

Amanda has a few of them.

A few years later, he and Davies attended Burnaby Central Secondary School as members of the Whitecaps academy. There was a large group of the Whitecaps kids who hung out with each other at school. They'd bring a big speaker and play music at lunchtime. Amanda remembered one time when the music just kept getting louder and louder, resulting in an impromptu dance party.

"We attracted a huge crowd," Amanda said. "The principal had to come and shut it all down. And Alphonso was in the middle of it. Literally, in the centre of it.

"He just loved entertaining people."

Amanda said Davies liked listening to rap music more than anything else. His favourite group was Migos, an African American hip hop trio from Georgia. He blasted Migos at home, in the locker rooms, everywhere.

"Oh my god," Amanda laughed. "At the time, it annoyed me."

When Davies first moved to Vancouver, he and Amanda lived in the same billet home. Amanda described it as a "disciplinary" environment, which he thought was tough on Davies. They weren't usually on the same schedules, as they were a part of different age groups, so they didn't spend a lot of time together at home. But they were supposed to eat dinner around 6:30 every night.

"Sometimes, I'd be texting him, 'Hey bro, should we have dinner? Where are you?'" Amanda recalled. "He's like, 'Nah I'm at the soccer field.' Or, 'Hey bro, I'm still at the mall right now with some of my friends. I'll be home late.' Stuff like that maybe made his first experience a bit difficult."

Lorrie Hansen remembered hearing from her daughter, Kaela, that Davies's billet parents were moving and the Whitecaps were struggling to find new options.

Kaela was a member of the Whitecaps' Girls Elite program, which had a similar structure to the men's academy. She was the same age as Davies and also attended Burnaby Central. Lorrie's son, Kyle, went to the school and was part of the Whitecaps academy as well, though he was two years younger.

Lorrie and her husband, Ed, both used to play soccer themselves. Lorrie played for Langara College in Vancouver, while Ed won a national championship at the University of New Brunswick.

Kaela and Davies got to talking about the idea of him living with their family. They all figured it would be a good arrangement. But they couldn't have expected it would have been *this* good.

"That kind of friendship happens once in a lifetime," Lorrie said.

The biggest thing, according to Lorrie, was that all the kids had the same energy. They were always on the go. They'd kick a ball around outside, play basketball or ping pong, go for runs — anything active. Then, of course, there was the dancing.

There was *always* dancing.

"You know the game *Just Dance*? That's where it started," Lorrie said. "I don't know if it was a Wii or an Xbox, but they all loved it. Spontaneously, they would just hop in front of the TV, turn on music, and start dancing. The music's in their blood. You turn it on, they start dancing."

While Kaela always liked dancing, Lorrie figures that Kyle got into it because of Davies. In addition to the spontaneous *Just Dance* sessions, he and Kyle would do all sorts of dance challenges and post them to Snapchat or Instagram. They even started a joint Instagram account, akdance.

These days, Kyle is a social media personality in his own right, with more than one million followers on TikTok. Kaela, who went on to play varsity soccer at the University of Kansas, is active on TikTok as well. Lorrie even has her own account.

In many ways, it was a match made in heaven.

"They were just so comfortable with each other," Lorrie said. "He was never shy around us, but he definitely showed his personality more around his peers."

Davies had his own room downstairs. It was a two-level house, and his room was by the front door, so it was almost as if he had his own little apartment. His friends would come in and out regularly. Lorrie said Davies and her children would pull typical teenage shenanigans every so often, like breaking curfews, but she always felt comfort in knowing that they were together and had each other's backs.

"He was having a normal life, and yet he had to maintain a public image. That was difficult for that age, I think," she said. "I've never seen him drink. Being high school kids, some of them did. He was probably the only one that didn't, I would say. But there were never really any issues."

Davies quickly became part of the family. He called Lorrie's sister "Tita," which means "aunty" in Filipino — Lorrie is a second-generation Canadian whose parents immigrated from the Philippines. And he always tried to include everybody, like the German exchange student who lived in their home when he first moved in.

In that sense, Lorrie said, her family learned a lot from Davies.

"He's just so open and welcoming," she said, also referencing Davies's generosity with his own personal belongings. "He can brighten up the room, but he's also very humble. He brought a lot of things to our family that made us appreciate what life is."

Davies was standing alone in front of the entire gymnasium.

It was a year-end Christmas concert at St. Nicholas Catholic Junior High. There were hundreds of faces in the crowd — students, teachers, parents.

144

In 2020, Davies became the first North American to be selected to the FIFA FIFPRO World 11, a prestigious list consisting of the world's best 11 players in a given season.

Davies signed a lucrative contract extension with Bayern amid his historic 2020 season . . . and a global pandemic.

"He comes at you full speed, you stand no chance."
— Pa-Modou Kah, coach and former defender

"If he or a teammate loses the ball, he's really quick in his head to switch modes and fight to get the ball back."

— Marco Neppe, Bayern technical director

Davies and Senegalese superstar Sadio Mané.

In April 2022, Bayern won their whopping 10th straight Bundesliga title.

Davies with legendary German goalkeeper Manuel Neuer and good friend Joshua Zirkzee.

Bayern sporting director Hasan Salihamidžić played an integral role in bringing Davies to Bayern.

When Bayern signed Davies, they wanted to make sure that he "never loses his smile."

Davies has been part of Canada's national team system since age 14.

On June 6, 2017, in Vancouver, Davies became a Canadian citizen . . .

. . . and earned his first call-up to the men's national team.

At age 16, Davies became the youngest player to play for the Canadian men's national team.

Two of the best to have donned the Maple Leaf: Davies and Atiba Hutchinson.

Davies scored two goals vs. French Guiana on July 7, 2017, becoming the youngest goalscorer in Canadian men's national team history.

At the 2018 FIFA Congress in Russia, Davies, Brianna Pinto, and Diego Lainez each delivered speeches on behalf of North America's successful bid for the 2026 FIFA World Cup.

"When Alphonso spoke, it just became a done deal. It was inevitable."
— John Herdman, Canadian men's national team head coach

Canada's "Golden Boys," Davies and Jonathan David.

Davies led Canada to their first win over the U.S. in 34 years, scoring the game-winning goal on October 15, 2019, at BMO Field.

Davies with longtime friend and teammate Sam Adekugbe.

The BMO Field crowd erupted after Davies's remarkable end-to-end goal vs. Panama in World Cup qualifying on October 13, 2021.

One of the most iconic moments in Canadian men's national team history.

"I think that really instilled him with a lot of confidence that he is the leader of this team. He is the best player. He could be the one that could take us there."
— Alistair Johnston, Canada defender

Edmonton fans welcomed Davies home for a World Cup qualifier vs. Costa Rica on November 12, 2021.

It was Davies's first game in Edmonton since leaving home at age 14. Think he was excited?

The "Iceteca" was born on November 16, 2021, as Canada defeated Mexico 2–1 on a snowy November day in Edmonton.

CANADA SOCCER, BEAU CHEVALIER

CANADA SOCCER, BEAU CHEVALIER

Davies was the first men's soccer player to win the Northern Star Award (formerly the Lou Marsh Trophy) as Canada's top athlete.

UNHCR/FC BAYERN MÜNCHEN

UNHCR/FC BAYERN MÜNCHEN

He was also the first Canadian and first soccer player to be appointed a Goodwill Ambassador for UNHCR, the UN Refugee Agency.

"I believe my personal story can help make a difference in people's lives," he told a round-table of international journalists following his appointment.

And like he so often does, Davies stole the show.

"It was off the cuff, nothing was scripted, and he started acting like, I think it was Barack Obama," Marco Bossio said. "He was doing some sort of improv in front of everybody. It was just remarkable how this kid was doing this without being afraid."

Unsurprisingly, Davies took drama at St. Nicholas, where his personality shone through like it did on that day. But the reality is that Davies's personality shone through in all sorts of situations.

During one congregation, he was one of a handful of students standing up, clapping his hands, and vibing to "Oh Happy Day" as everyone else in the gymnasium remained seated. It didn't matter who was watching. It was like Davies had not a care in the world.

That attitude followed him wherever he went.

"Even with something as dry as math, he made it lively and fun," Bossio said.

There was nothing like his energy around the soccer team, though. That's where Davies really came alive. Bossio would drive the team to games in a bus decked out in the school's red, black, and white colours. They called it the "Knight Rider," a reference to their team name, the Knights. Davies would be on the bus singing, dancing, cracking jokes — whatever it took to get the boys going.

Similarly, with the Strikers, Talal Al-Awaid remembered having to rent a couple of 15-passenger vans for the team when they were away at the Dallas Cup. Once Davies got into one, everyone else seemed to follow him.

They knew what was coming.

"You can hear them in the back, you look over, and they're just having these freestyle battles," Al-Awaid said. "He was the one initiating it. He was always the one trying to get it going . . . He never took himself too seriously. He'd make fun of himself a bit and get guys laughing. He was never shy. Whatever the situation was, he liked that spotlight and he seemed to thrive under that spotlight . . . You see a lot more of it now on his social media and stuff, but he was doing that before he even had a phone."

Davies was made for social media.

One of the first platforms he used was ASKfm, a Q&A service

145

that encouraged users to submit questions anonymously. He was also an early adopter of Snapchat.

By age 21, he could be found on Facebook, Instagram, Snapchat, TikTok, Twitch, Twitter, and YouTube. Between Instagram and TikTok alone, he had more than 11 million followers. On most of his posts, he signed off with #AD19 and a lightning bolt emoji, his own personal brand.

This isn't your typical athlete-cliché type stuff, either. On his Snapchat profile, Davies's bio reads "Don't forget to smile today." It's hard not to when perusing his content.

In one TikTok video, Davies re-enacted the scene from *Brooklyn Nine-Nine* where the detective, played by Andy Samberg, has five suspects in a police lineup recite the lyrics to Backstreet Boys hit "I Want It That Way." Davies brilliantly imitated each of them, with costume changes and all, and spliced everything together in a hilarious one-minute package.

In another viral video, Davies prank-called some of his friends and Bayern Munich teammates via FaceTime. Right after they answered, Davies would say "I can't talk right now, let me call you back" before cackling over their puzzled reactions.

Davies first started using TikTok right at the end of 2019. When the pandemic hit in March 2020, he became even more active. Like many others, he was stuck at home with more time on his hands. TikTok was a way to keep himself, and others, entertained.

Early on during the pandemic, he posted a video of himself running away from the "Coronavirus." Naturally, being in isolation, he played both roles.

"Ha ha, loser," Davies said as he locked himself in a car. "You ain't gonna catch me, fam."

"Hey fam, catch you next time," he responded as the hooded virus.

While TikTok is where most of Davies's comedic content can be found, he's also active on other channels.

After winning the Champions League, Davies responded to a congratulatory message from the Canadian Prime Minister with a tweet that read "Thank you Prime Minister @JustinTrudeau! Can I please come home for a week?" with praying hands, the grimacing face, and three Canadian flags — a cheeky reference to Canada's border restrictions during the pandemic.

On Instagram, he'll often go live with friends and interact with his thousands of viewers. One time, he claimed to give out his phone number. But it was actually the number of a friend, whose phone subsequently blew up with non-stop messages and calls.

On Twitch, he'll stream himself playing video games like *FIFA* and *Call of Duty*.

On YouTube, where he was particularly active during his first year in Germany, he did a *Cribs*-style house tour, something called a "mukbang" where he told the story of his career while eating sushi, and several streeter-style interviews where he approached strangers on the streets of Munich and asked them all sorts of fun and random questions like a seasoned TV host. During one of his outings, he even spotted a young kid wearing a Davies Bayern jersey.

"I just saw the coolest thing ever," he said. "Look at this. Shout-out to this little homie!"

Before they split up in the spring of 2022, Davies also had a joint YouTube vlog with girlfriend Jordyn Huitema. Like Davies, Huitema came through the Vancouver Whitecaps youth system and represented the Canadian national team at a young age before moving to Europe, where she joined Paris Saint-Germain Féminine in France. She and Davies started dating in Vancouver and gave fans a glimpse of their continued relationship while living in the neighbouring European countries. Their fun-loving videos, which included baking challenges, gingerbread house competitions, and trips to Disneyland Paris, averaged about two million views per episode.

Davies has an editor for some of his more polished videos, such as his soccer highlight reels. For a while, he used a good friend from Vancouver. But he produces most of his own content, especially the fun and creative pieces, and edits his own YouTube vlogs. For those, he used iMovie when he was first starting out before upgrading to Adobe Premiere Pro.

"He likes editing," said Kassim Khimji, who works closely with Davies as the head of media and marketing at ATG Sports Management, a boutique sports agency that Huoseh founded. "I've told him, 'Hey, Alphonso, if you need someone to do thumbnails for you and YouTube edits, let me know.' He's like, 'Nah, it's cool. I like doing it. It's fun. It's like my distraction from soccer.'"

Khimji has a little bit of a history with Davies himself. He used to coach against his Strikers teams during Davies's youth soccer days in Edmonton and create entire game plans around trying to stop him. They rarely worked. Khimji further developed his relationship with Davies during his stint as a communications intern with the Whitecaps, which overlapped with Davies's final season at the club. After holding communications and marketing roles with FC Edmonton and Olympia Sports International, he then joined up with Huoseh at ATG Sports.

Most of their in-depth planning and collaborative sessions with Davies take place around the kitchen table when he's back in Edmonton during the summer and Christmas holidays. But Khimji and Davies also stay in touch throughout the year, shooting each other ideas and voice notes over WhatsApp.

"He's not a picky guy," Khimji said. "If we ask him, 'Hey Phonzie, are you OK with this?' Most of the time it's 'Yeah, that's cool with me.' There are no ifs or buts or stresses."

Khimji's priorities at ATG Sports include media and public relations, marketing and brand strategy, sponsorship and endorsement, and social media management — he'll help run Davies's channels with things like graphic design, promotional posts, monitoring, and other routine tasks. But most of what you see on Davies's channels is just Davies being himself.

"And that's how we want it to be," Khimji said. "Because you see a lot of athletes out there, when they hit a certain level of success, they kind of turn into robots, you know? They became too commercialized. With Alphonso, he's just a very authentic, genuine kid. He's Alphonso. He's himself. He doesn't change who he is."

That can come with its own risks.

For instance, Davies once made an off-handed comment on Twitch suggesting Cristiano Ronaldo should be the captain at Manchester United instead of Harry Maguire. A regular fan or pundit could have said the exact same thing without anyone batting an eye. Because

Davies said it, it naturally made headlines around the world and upset a portion of the fan base.

"People follow you because they want to see who you are," Khimji said. "OK, once in a while, you post some stupid shit, no problem. I look at my Facebook memories when I was 20 years old, and there's some cringe stuff on there. Why should it be any different for Alphonso? . . . When he's 25 or 26, he's going to look back and say, man, that TikTok, what was I thinking? But that's part of the experience of being a human being, having those moments. You don't want to take that away from him by saying, 'Hey Alphonso, don't post this, hey Alphonso, don't post that, oh this YouTube idea is stupid.' Let him do things. Because that's authentic to him and his personality in that moment."

And it's a big part of the reason brands love him. As a world-class athlete with an incredible backstory and a colourful personality, Davies is a marketer's dream. It's no wonder so many companies wanted to associate with him from a young age.

By age 21, he'd had endorsement deals with Nike, EA Sports, BMO, Crocs, BioSteel, Topps Trading Cards, Konami (the developer for popular video game series *Pro Evolution Soccer*), and Binance — a world-leading cryptocurrency exchange through which Davies had his very own non-fungible token (NFT) collection created.

And interest from many, many others.

"The thing that really got companies reaching out wasn't necessarily his success with the Champions League and Bayern and winning those six trophies," Khimji said. "It was actually mainly from his TikTok. A lot of companies saw his TikTok and they said, 'Wow, man, this kid is good. He can market and he can sell a product.' So they wanted him to market and sell their product. And they're like, 'Oh, it'd be great if we did a deal and he could make some funny TikToks.' It's like you can't expect the kid to just be a robot and dance or something. It has to be authentic to him and he'll make good content around it."

Naturally, there's a financial component to most of these partnerships. If they're lucky, an athlete's career might last 10 to 15 years. It's important that they capitalize on that window financially, by creating multiple revenue streams, to set them up for future success.

And in Davies's case, he's not just thinking about himself.

"At the end of the day, his whole family relies on him," Khimji said. "It's not just Alphonso looking out for himself and his mom, his dad, brother, and sister. It's his aunts, and his cousins, and everyone. We recognize the importance of that. That's why we try to get good commercial deals that value him."

At the same time, they won't just do a deal with anyone. They prefer a quality over quantity approach, especially considering these deals often come with various media and content obligations that require a significant time commitment. And, perhaps most importantly, they're only interested in brands that align with Davies's values and interests.

"Alphonso loves Nike, so we work with Nike," Khimji said. "We did a deal with Crocs because Alphonso loves Crocs. So it's a way of showing your personality to the world."

The deal with Nike was actually done before Davies made the move to Bayern.

In 2018, he was featured in the Emmy-winning Nike commercial, narrated by Colin Kaepernick, that was seen around the world. The two-minute spot, titled "Dream Crazy," centred on overcoming adversity to achieve greatness, telling the stories of LeBron James, Serena Williams, and other inspirational athletes.

Right before LeBron's scene, Davies appeared.

"If you're born a refugee, don't let it stop you from playing soccer, for the national team, at age 16," Kaepernick narrated over footage of Davies scoring for Canada.

The commercial dropped when Davies was on the bus with the Canadian national team heading to training. A lot of the players watched it on their phones simultaneously.

"He was a superstar to us, but now at that point, I think he transitioned to a superstar globally," Teibert said. "That was really cool. He was in the same commercial and held in the same light as these dominant forces in their craft. We were all just kind of in awe on the bus. Then there's Alphonso, just kind of taking it in stride.

150

It's like another day for him. He goes on the field after that and he's just the same Alphonso training, nothing's different."

That's the thing about Davies.

He doesn't do it for fame, followers, sponsorship deals, or anything else. Those things are just a natural by-product of the type of person he is and everything he's accomplished.

"Maybe people see on social media that he's this fun whatever, but he's not the Kei [Kamara] or Chad Ochocinco that loves the media and jumps on it and wants all the fame and the press," Kamara said, adding that Davies seemed "ashamed" of the attention he was getting back in 2018.

"He's not that guy."

And if you ask Khimji, he probably never will be.

As comfortable as Davies appears on his own social media channels, it's not usually the case when he's in front of the media or working with partners behind the scenes. In those types of settings, Khimji said, it'll usually take him at least half an hour to start coming out of his shell.

"A lot of people think Alphonso is just this vibrant kid 24/7, but he's actually very quiet," Khimji said. "He still definitely has that to him. It hasn't changed. And I don't see it changing ever, to be honest."

The 2018 Nike commercial, and in particular the prominence of Kaepernick, was controversial to say the least. The former San Francisco 49ers quarterback was revered by some and shunned by others for his decision to kneel during the U.S. national anthem in protest of racial injustice and police brutality.

Regardless, the inclusion of Davies in such a high-profile campaign was a sign of things to come.

"He's so unique because he's a North American star playing in Europe that's from Africa," Khimji said. "So you have three of the biggest demographics in the world that he connects to organically. I think he has potential to be one of the most marketable soccer players, eventually. I think he's getting there. We've had other people approach us, people that represent the biggest stars in the NBA, the LeBron James of the world, their management teams, they reach out to us and say, 'This kid is like a billion-dollar industry.'

Maybe a billion dollars is a bit of a stretch, but I definitely think he can be one of the most marketable athletes in North America by 2026."

Maybe even sooner.

A 2021 study conducted by Toronto-based marketing consultancy IMI International, in partnership with TSN, listed Davies as the most marketable Canadian athlete worldwide.

"IMI International's survey, believed to be the first of its kind, examined how aware respondents around the world were of active Canadian athletes, their likeability, and whether respondents would want to meet the athletes and support the brands they endorse. The survey also explored professional athletes' level of engagement on social media platforms, as well as how many internet searches were done for each athlete," leading investigative journalist Rick Westhead wrote on TSN.ca, adding that the survey was based on more than 112,000 respondents in 150 countries across North America, Europe, and Asia.

Though Davies topped the list of the most marketable Canadian athletes on a global scale, he didn't even crack the top 15 when only Canadian respondents were considered.

Unsurprisingly, that list was dominated by NHL players.

"His biggest weakness right now from the marketing side is that not enough people in Canada and USA know him," Khimji said, while acknowledging that an appearance at the World Cup could change that in a hurry.

So what's next?

In the coming years, Khimji said, people might start to see Davies spending some time in Africa during the offseasons and connecting more with that part of his fan base.

"He really wants to go back home to Africa — to Ghana and Liberia," Khimji said. "He's really embracing his African roots more and more as he gets older."

Additionally, they might see a more "business-minded" Davies who showcases his passion for the arts in different ways. Davies loves fashion and music, so there's a good chance he'll get into those spaces. He's already been singing, rapping, and producing music as part of Stugang, a band he formed with a couple of friends and fellow footballers in Germany. In one song, he said being in the studio was his "therapy."

"He stopped playing a lot of video games. Instead of playing video games, he's in his 'lab,'" Khimji said, referencing a tech room Davies set up in his Munich home. "And whether it's editing videos or creating music, he's always playing with software now."

Davies has also expressed his desire, publicly, to become an actor down the road. Growing up, he enjoyed watching *The Fresh Prince of Bel-Air* and in particular Will Smith. He's also cited *Rush Hour* as one of his favourite movies. Neither of which should come as a surprise considering his sense of humour.

For now, Davies said he's hoping there are "a lot of soccer years" ahead of him. That's his focus, though he did admit the "entertainment business" may be his calling after soccer. Whatever happens, those close to Davies are sure of one thing.

He's not going to change. As he said in Bayern's club magazine, "Life is too short to be angry or sad for long." So he's going to continue living every day like it's his last.

"I don't think it would matter whatever cards he was dealt," Teibert said. "He would make the best out of whatever cards he was holding. And he would still have a smile on his face."

CHAPTER 13:
HISTORY OF HEARTBREAK

A win or a draw against Honduras was all Canada needed.
It was their sixth attempt at qualifying for the FIFA World Cup, the pinnacle of the sport. Their five previous attempts — in 1958, 1970, 1974, 1978, and 1982 — had come to nothing.

On CBC's broadcast, head coach Tony Waiters called it the most important game that Canada had ever played. And it would be played on September 14, 1985 . . . in St. John's, Newfoundland.

Wait, what?

Not Toronto? Not Vancouver? Not Montreal?

Sitting along the North Atlantic Ocean on an island carved in rock, St. John's is the easternmost city in North America, excluding Greenland. It's closer to London, England, than it is to Edmonton.

Let that sink in for a second.

A lot of people outside of Canada wouldn't have even heard of it. They certainly wouldn't be able to point to it on a map. It's perhaps for that reason a couple hundred Honduran fans, as legend has it, instead travelled to Saint John, New Brunswick, and ended up missing the game.

There were commercial implications to hosting the game in St. John's — Waiters told Sportsnet years later that Canada Soccer had a "financial guarantee" from the Newfoundland and Labrador Soccer Association. But there was also a little gamesmanship at play.

Whenever Canada played in Central America, they were forced to endure the sweltering heat. Three weeks earlier, Honduras had hosted Canada in the capital city of Tegucigalpa and scheduled the game at 3 p.m., the hottest time of the day, to make it as hard as possible on the Canadians.

The thinking was that wet and windy St. John's, known for its harsh weather, could have the reverse effect. And the Hondurans, who flew in two days before the game, got a taste of it right away.

"It was a miserable day," Carl Valentine said. "And we were happy about that."

Valentine had only just obtained his Canadian citizenship the year prior after spending five seasons with the Vancouver Whitecaps in the old NASL. But when the league folded, he returned to his birth country and joined West Bromwich Albion in the English First Division. That's when he first got an invite to represent the Canadian national team at the 1984 Olympics, where they'd go on to reach the quarterfinal.

Having just returned to England, he respectfully declined.

"Great decision," he said sarcastically.

On the heels of their Olympic run, Canada began their qualifying campaign for the 1986 FIFA World Cup in April 1985. Valentine didn't get the call for any of the first seven games, so he was shocked when the phone rang prior to that September afternoon in St. John's.

"I think they had some injuries just before the last game against Honduras," Valentine said. "So Tony Waiters called me up and asked if I'd like to play in the game."

He wasn't going to make the same mistake twice.

Valentine said he felt "apprehensive" as he travelled to St. John's.

He wasn't sure how he'd be received by his teammates after turning down Canada in the Olympics. And then, to make matters worse, he got sick on the way there.

He called it "Montezuma's revenge."

Google it.

"I was in bed most of the week," Valentine said. "It was coming out of both sides."

But Valentine pulled himself together, managed to train once or twice, and was in the starting lineup as Canada walked onto the old grass field at King George V Park, a rustic 60-year-old venue that looked and felt more like a city park than it did a proper soccer stadium.

Even the location of the field itself was rather unique.

Those who approached the entrance from the south, along Lake Avenue or Clancey Drive, passed a cemetery. Those who came from The Boulevard on the north passed a different one. In between the two cemeteries sat little King George V Park, resting at the head of the picturesque Quidi Vidi Lake.

Temporary bleachers were brought in to enclose the field, creating an intimate feel, though a smattering of trees, parked cars, and houses were still visible. At one point, the game paused for over a minute as officials tried to recover an errant ball that flew over the bleachers and into the parking lot.

It's not what anyone would have expected for a game of such magnitude, but the Newfoundlanders certainly didn't care. They started filling the stadium two hours before kickoff and gave the Canadians a standing ovation during warmup. Some reports had the attendance around 8,000. Others claimed it was closer to 13,000. Either way, it was well above the official capacity. And that doesn't even factor in those who were watching from their houses along The Boulevard.

There were Canadian flags *everywhere*.

"Just walking out in front of that crowd was phenomenal," Valentine said. "I came from West Bromwich. I got to play at the theatre of dreams at Old Trafford, at Highbury, where Arsenal played. I mean, I played in Azteca with 100,000, and it's tough to beat. But the atmosphere there was just electric. That crowd, and the energy, I think really willed us on that game."

Canada won 2–1. Valentine delivered the corner kicks that led to both goals.

Fans stormed the field at the final whistle.

"O Canada" could be heard blaring from the Canadian locker room shortly thereafter.

With Mexico hosting the 1986 World Cup, thereby earning automatic qualification, there was only one spot up for grabs amongst the 17 remaining teams competing in Concacaf (the Confederation of North, Central America and Caribbean Association Football).

And it belonged to Canada.

"That was the best moment of our lives," said Paul Dolan, Canada's backup goalkeeper on the day.

"There was nothing high-end professional about the pitch, the stadium, the dressing room. It's basically a recreational park that we were at. But you've got a bunch of guys that had just achieved something that no other Canadian team had done. And it couldn't have been a better place for us to all celebrate it."

Dolan ended up starting Canada's first game at the World Cup. They were up against France, a superpower who had just won the most recent Euros. A superpower led by Michel Platini, who had just been awarded the Ballon d'Or as the best player in the world in three straight years.

Nobody gave Canada a chance.

On the way to the stadium, Dolan remembered seeing the host Mexican fans holding up their fingers with different numbers. Four. Five. Six. Seven. Eight.

"The numbers up of how many goals they thought we were going to concede," Dolan said.

In the end, it was only one.

Canada held their own and fell to a 1–0 defeat after conceding a late 79th-minute goal. They lost their next two games against Hungary and Russia, too, both by a scoreline of 2–0. Although they failed to score a goal or earn a result, Canada certainly didn't embarrass themselves. Especially in that first game against France, and in the Olympics a year prior, they showed they could compete with the best.

It felt like the beginning of something special.

"At the age of 20, I thought that I could play in five World Cups," Dolan chuckled, knowing what he knows now. "As a young player, you feel, of course, we're going to be back here again."

It didn't quite go as planned.

It's impossible to talk about the impact Davies has made on the Canadian men's national team without understanding its turbulent history.

Mexico '86 was an important milestone for the program. It certainly helped inspire a new generation of Canadian soccer fans and players alike. Some of them went on to play for the national team and win the 2000 Concacaf Gold Cup, one of the program's greatest accomplishments to date. But for years, whenever anyone mentioned '86, it would inevitably come with a qualifier.

"That one time Canada made it to the World Cup," one CBC headline put it.

People hoped it'd be a harbinger.

Instead, it was an outlier.

It's an entirely different story for the women's national team, who consistently competed in World Cups and reached three consecutive Olympic podiums culminating with a historic gold medal in 2021. They carried the torch for soccer in Canada for a long time, while facing many of the same challenges as the men's team, if not more, and connected with the country in a way few sports teams ever have. Maybe ever will.

But this is a nation with deep, painful scars on the men's side of the game.

So where exactly did things go wrong?

From Dolan's perspective, it all started with the demise of the NASL.

"I don't think people can overestimate the importance of that league," he said. "It was so important for the development of young Canadian players to be playing at a really high level, with some of the best players in the world, literally. David McGill didn't play on the national team, but he was playing alongside Johan Cruyff. Then you've got the Whitecaps playing alongside Alan Ball. You know, guys who have played in the World Cup, at the highest level. And there are a ton of stories of players like that sprinkled throughout the North American Soccer League."

Consider this: 18 of the 22 players on Canada's roster at the 1986 World Cup at one point plied their trade in the NASL, a U.S.-based professional league that also had some Canadian teams. It's not a coincidence. When the league folded, largely due to a financial collapse, there was no longer an infrastructure in place for professional Canadian players to develop and thrive.

"Right after the World Cup, really the only way to make a living in soccer was to play in the indoor league, which wasn't even beneficial to the outdoor game," Dolan said.

Many Canadians were left scrambling.

Dolan went off to the UK and tried to get a job there. He impressed on a trial at Sheffield Wednesday, who were competing in England's top division, but things fell through after he failed to obtain a work permit. That was, and remains to be, a real challenge for Canadians and other foreigners without European lineage. Not to mention, at that period, the English leagues were very much . . . English.

"I became friends with the Icelandic international at Sheffield Wednesday because we were the only two who weren't English," said Dolan, who got the nickname "Moose" from his teammates.

It was an uphill battle.

In England, there was the challenge of obtaining a work permit. And Dolan said Canadians didn't really have a connection or pathway to the other European leagues. It's not like there was a lot of interest in Canadian players, anyway, even after their World Cup appearance.

"I remember Dale Mitchell, who was a phenomenal player, went over. John Catliff as well," Valentine said. "And they just weren't really getting looked at. It was kind of like you had to go over and not just be better, but really three, four times better than the young players that they had over there."

There were those that made it.

Craig Forrest played more than 300 games in England, mostly with Ipswich Town FC. Notably, he was one of just 13 foreigners who featured on the opening weekend of the English Premier League in 1992.

Frank Yallop also had a great tenure at Ipswich during the same period, as did Jason de Vos years later following successful stints with Dundee United FC and Wigan Athletic FC.

Randy Samuel, a member of the '86 World Cup squad, played in the top division in the Netherlands.

Alex Bunbury became the all-time leading goalscorer for top-flight Portuguese club CS Marítimo.

Paul Stalteri won the Bundesliga and German Cup with SV Werden Bremen.

Julian de Guzman was the first Canadian to play in La Liga, Spain's top league.

And there were others.

But they were the exception. Not the rule.

The demise of the NASL and the lack of opportunities for Canadian players following the 1986 World Cup led to the creation of the Canadian Soccer League (CSL). Most countries around the world already had their own domestic league.

Now Canada did too.

"And I think that gave us a really good chance, but it wasn't the same as having a major professional soccer league," said Dolan, who played in the CSL with the Vancouver 86ers and Hamilton Steelers before the league folded after six seasons. "That's part of it. There are a million other reasons."

Canada Soccer has taken its fair share of blame, with many former players pointing to a lack of professionalism within the governing body.

But even then, some of it came down to bad luck.

In the next cycle of World Cup qualifying following 1986, Canada had a home-and-away series against Guatemala to advance to the final stage. After losing 1–0 in Guatemala, Canada won 3–2 in the second leg but failed to advance by virtue of the away-goals tiebreaker after conceding what Dolan called "one of the most unlucky goals ever."

"[The defender] went to clear it at the edge of the 18, it hit the player's shin, and looped over my head into the goal," Dolan recounted in agony.

Then in qualifying for the 1994 World Cup, which would be hosted in the U.S., Canada did in fact advance to the final round and finished second only to Mexico, resulting in a playoff against Australia. But they came up ever so short once again, this time in a penalty shootout.

"One thing or another seemed to be a stumbling block along the way," Dolan said.

At the end of the day, most agree that Canada simply wasn't good enough. They didn't have the quality, belief, or support to overcome these challenges.

One of the biggest ones?

Playing on the road in the Concacaf region, particularly in Mexico and soccer-crazed Central American countries like Costa Rica, El Salvador, Honduras, and Panama. These are the national teams Canada had to beat to qualify for a World Cup. Aside from Mexico and maybe Costa Rica, they might not scare anyone from a pure sporting standpoint.

But there's way more to it than meets the eye.

"It's life and death down there for a lot of these countries and teams," David Edgar said.

He would know, having played 42 games for the Canadian men's national team.

"Don't get me wrong, I've had good experiences," Edgar said of his travels around Concacaf. "And bad experiences. More bad than good."

Imagine trying to sleep the night before a big game only to have hundreds of fans camped outside your hotel doing everything they can to keep you awake — chanting, revving motorcycle engines, setting off fireworks, honking horns, sounding sirens, banging drums, and playing music all through the night.

That happened in Panama, as police officers and hotel staff looked on.

"They're doing nothing to move the fans away," Edgar said. "And the hotel has put us right at the front of the hotel. The back would have actually been quiet, because it's a courtyard."

Imagine being escorted into a stadium by police officers wielding machine guns, playing on a bumpy field surrounded by barbed wire, and having all sorts of projectiles thrown at you from the rowdy crowd — limes in Costa Rica, big heavy jugs of water in Honduras, bags of urine in El Salvador.

That all happened too.

Imagine trying to breathe, let alone run around and play soccer, in the tropical heat with temperatures exceeding 40 degrees Celsius and humidity that makes it feel even hotter.

That almost always happened.

And those are just the Coles Notes.

"All those stories are true," said Dolan, who experienced it first as a player and then as Canada's goalkeeper coach for many years thereafter. "Truthfully, in some sense, it's kind of fun. You know you're in something that means so much to everyone. But when you're younger, it can be intimidating. And it can also be dangerous. It can make you feel inferior when you step on the pitch."

And all those things came to roost on October 16, 2012.

Once again, a win or draw against Honduras was all Canada needed.

Unlike in 1985, a World Cup berth wasn't on the line quite yet. Rather, this game would determine which team advanced to the Hexagonal, or the Hex, the final round of World Cup qualifying featuring the last six teams standing in Concacaf. Get to the Hex, and the World Cup is within reach.

Canada hadn't made it that far since 1997.

Considering how long it had been, the stakes felt as high as they did all those years ago in St. John's. Only this time, the game wouldn't be played in St. John's. It would be played in San Pedro Sula, a Honduran city that had just been labeled the "Murder Capital of the World."

Up until that point, the stories of Canada competing in Central America were just that.

Stories.

There wasn't a lot of media coverage. Social media wasn't what it is today. A lot of times, Dolan said, Canada's travelling party would only be around 20 people, including staff.

It was hard to get people to understand what it was like in those hostile environments.

You had to be there.

"The first time I really think that it struck home was when Arash Madani and Kurt Larson went down," Dolan said, referencing the trip to San Pedro Sula in October 2012. "They really got a sense of what this thing was all about."

Larson was a writer for the *Toronto Sun* at the time. The day before the game, he wrote a story about the Estadio Olímpico Metropolitano, which would host the decisive qualifier. He described the stadium as "intimidating and menacing," thanks in part to the barbed-wire fencing that surrounded the field as an extra layer of security between the players and fans.

Madani was sent down as a sideline reporter for Sportsnet, the television network that would be broadcasting the game across Canada. It was the first time he'd travelled to Central America, or anywhere outside of Canada and the U.S., to cover soccer.

He didn't quite know what he was getting into.

A few days before he left, he got a bit of a heads-up from Forrest, a Sportsnet colleague and former goalkeeper who played 56 games with the Canadian men's national team.

But it still didn't compute.

"I didn't even know what he was talking about," Madani recalled. "It's not that I was dismissing it. I just didn't get it. Like, what do you mean you were stuck in the locker room, there was riot police outside, and then you guys had to sneak onto the bus after like 90 minutes, and they were throwing rocks at the bus, shaking the bus, and the bus driver just made an executive decision to hammer on the gas and if people were in the way, well, that's the cost of doing business. Like, what do you mean?

"Then I got there and I'm like, 'Oh shit, now I see.'"

As a member of the official broadcaster, Madani flew to San Pedro Sula with the team on a charter. He remembered speaking to de Guzman, one of Canada's experienced midfielders, at the terminal.

After some pleasantries, de Guzman dropped a bombshell.

"If we win or tie on Tuesday, my brother's going to come play in the Hex and so is Junior Hoilett," Madani remembered him saying.

De Guzman's younger brother, Jonathan, was a highly rated midfielder playing for Swansea City in the English Premier League. He was born in Canada but also had Dutch citizenship and had previously expressed his desire to represent the Oranje rather than Les Rouges.

Hoilett, a fellow English Premier League player, was in a similar boat.

At the time, these were two of the most hyped Canadian-born players in the world. Getting one of them for the World Cup run would be a big deal. Getting both of them?

163

A home run.

"Are you serious?" Madani asked de Guzman.

"I can put my life on that," he reiterated, this time on camera, the night before the game.

The game would be played at 2 p.m. on Tuesday afternoon. A national holiday previously scheduled for Monday had been pushed to Tuesday so Hondurans could watch.

After breakfast, Madani made his way to the stadium with his Sportsnet crew and other members of the Canadian media, including Larson, Neil Davidson from the Canadian Press, and Daniel Girard from the *Toronto Star*. They sat in silence as they peered out the windows, observing the developing scene.

"Everyone's going to the stadium. It's just like paddy wagons, pickup trucks full of people. All of it," Madani said. "I'd never seen anything like this before. Then you walk into the stadium, everyone's there three hours early. The whole place is just chanting, 'Hon-du-ras, Hon-du-ras!' People are, like, hanging from the rafters, on top of the awning, over the seats. There's barbed wire everywhere. There's machine guns and riot police. It was hot, humid, and intimidating as fuck."

Edgar remembered it taking around 30 minutes for Canada's team bus to navigate the crowd of fans surrounding the stadium and pull into the entrance next to the visitor's locker room. The buzz of the crowd and their synchronized horns was already deafening. Edgar was on the phone with his wife as he got off the bus, but his signal dropped once he entered the stadium.

Madani and his crew were also having technical difficulties.

"Our technical producer came out, he put his palms on my shoulder blades, and he said, 'Buddy, here's the deal. We have no monitor, we have no return feed, we have no clock, we have no communication with Toronto. But we have a wire going through a banana tree into a minivan, and I think we'll be able to go live from here,'" Madani recalled.

When it was finally time for kickoff, the players walked onto the field through a dark and narrow tunnel that felt like it was literally shaking from the fans above them.

"It's all pitch-black aside from this one little crack at the top, where you can peer out and sunlight is coming in," Madani said. "And all you can see is barbed wire. And the fans just pound on this tin tunnel.

"I'm like, 'Oh boy.'"

Despite all of this, the first chance fell to Canada just one minute into the match. But they failed to connect on a cross at the top of the six-yard box, and Honduras came back the other way and scored five minutes later.

Canada nearly equalized immediately, firing a low strike off the post before having a point-blank rebound attempt saved by the Honduran goalkeeper. Once again, Honduras came back the other way and scored to make it 2–0.

"If you had any type of wavering going in, how do you recover from 2–0?" said Dolan, who was on the sideline as Canada's goalkeeper coach. "Mentally, that was so difficult for them. It just got worse and worse and worse. Every chance that we missed got magnified, and every goal that they scored got spurred on by that incredible crowd. That's where it just went south for us and north for them."

With Canada trailing 4–0 at halftime, Madani interviewed Canadian captain Kevin McKenna, who said live on Sportsnet that "it's all about damage limitation now."

But they couldn't stop the bleeding.

"It almost felt like they were all in quicksand and didn't know how to get out of it," Madani said.

The final score: Honduras 8. Canada 1.

It was Canada's worst defeat in nearly 20 years and yet another disappointing end to their hopes of getting back to a World Cup.

"All we could do is ask for the fans' forgiveness," Canada head coach Stephen Hart told Madani moments after the final whistle. "We know they probably won't forgive me, but forgive the players."

Madani said that whole day felt like an out-of-body experience. None of it felt real.

"I've been to college football games with 100,000 people, I've been to Super Bowls, I've been to World Series Game 7," he said. "I had never felt, seen, experienced anything like that."

Was Honduras *that* much better than Canada?

You could definitely make the argument that they were better. But seven goals better? Just four months earlier, the two teams played to a scoreless draw at BMO Field in Toronto. If Canada were to have won that game, they wouldn't have even needed any points in Honduras.

They would have been through.

"We knew, excuse my language, that we kind of fucked up at home by dropping points when we shouldn't have," Edgar said. "Honduras, the team we played at BMO, was not the same Honduras team we played down in San Pedro Sula. By any shape of the imagination. They're a different animal."

There were some extenuating circumstances at play. The legendary Dwayne De Rosario, who just a month earlier had become the all-time leading goalscorer for Canada's men's national team, was out injured. And a few other players got sick in the days leading up to the game. But this did nothing to save Canada from the humiliation that would ensue.

Canada flew back home later that night, mostly in stunned silence, and Edgar met up with his mom for lunch at a pub the next day. They were talking about the game on TSN.

He could barely watch.

"Obviously it was embarrassing no matter what way you look at it. It was an 8–1 loss," Edgar said. "But the way the media portrayed us after that was the laughingstock type thing. I think that stung the most. Getting back to England, I was at Burnley, and the players didn't really understand. They think playing for Canada at that time was a jolly up and blah blah blah. They're like, 'How the hell do you lose 8–1 to Honduras?' They don't see Honduras being a footballing nation. I'm like, 'Guys, come down there and see for yourself.' It was tough. It was tough. I've spoken to a few players, Atiba Hutchinson, Iain Hume, players that were involved in that. And for years, we found it hard to talk about."

And yet, for years, it was all anyone ever did.

Rightly or wrongly, it became a symbol of Canada's failures in the men's game.

Following the 8–1 loss in Honduras, they went nearly two years without winning a game and, at one point, 10 games without scoring a goal. During that stretch, their FIFA ranking dropped to 122nd in the world, an all-time low. They were changing coaches every year or two. Dual nationals, like the younger de Guzman, were committing to other countries. And a lot of the players on their roster weren't even employed, which became a running joke.

"People laughed at us because we were Unattached FC at times," Edgar said. "There were players who didn't have clubs coming into camps. I came from an era where I earned my first cap. It took me two years with camps and things like that. But I felt at times we threw out caps like frisbees too much."

Through it all, mainstream interest was essentially non-existent. Canada's diehard soccer supporters were forced to watch games on dodgy, illegal streams with commentators who went by Mad Bull and Maestro, and share in their misery over a national team that was once described as one of the most underachieving in world soccer.

As a result, some of the best players to have worn a Canadian national team jersey went largely unnoticed by the greater public. Like Hutchinson, who was Canada Soccer's men's player of the year six times and had an illustrious career in Europe.

Dolan described Hutchinson as a "heart and soul" type player who always showed up for his country. Even as he got older, even after he moved to Turkey to play for Beşiktaş.

But he never got the fanfare he deserved back home.

"Atiba Hutchinson is the best Canadian soccer player you've never heard of," a *Toronto Star* headline read in 2018.

Part of that was the nature of his game. He wasn't a flashy player. But it's hard not to imagine what could have been if Canada was able to get over the hump one of those years.

Not only for Hutchinson, but for the entire program.

"They'd gone so long without getting that close," Madani said of the perception around the team after that fateful afternoon in San Pedro Sula. "The feeling was they're doomed forever.

"Nobody saw a light at the end of the tunnel."

CHAPTER 14:
GOLDEN GENERATION

John Herdman called Davies in for a meeting the night before the game.

It had been 34 years since the Canadian men's national team had beaten the U.S.

Thirty-four.

In the build-up, Canada Soccer released a hype video showcasing a compilation of memorable sports moments between Canada and the U.S. Donovan Bailey crossing the finishing line ahead of the U.S. to win gold in the 4×100-metre relay at Atlanta 1996. Hayley Wickenheiser scoring in the gold medal game at Salt Lake 2002. Sidney Crosby's "Golden Goal" at Vancouver 2010. Christine Sinclair's hat-trick at London 2012.

The only men's soccer clip included?

A disallowed goal from Atiba Hutchinson, who was incorrectly called offside in the dying stages of the 2007 Gold Cup semifinal. If you ever hear Canadian supporters vehemently maintaining that "Atiba was onside," and it's a regular occurrence to this very day, that's why.

It was the closest thing they'd had to a real moment against the U.S.

Canada's last win over their southern neighbours came in 1985, the same year they qualified for the World Cup. And Herdman knew that Davies could be key to changing Canada's fortunes. But he also knew that the soon-to-be 19-year-old was going through a tough spell.

It was the fall of 2019. Davies was in the midst of his first full season at Bayern. He was struggling to get minutes. Prior to joining up with the national team, his last game was with Bayern's second team. Herdman felt like he wasn't playing with the freedom that he used to.

So he showed Davies some clips from his Whitecaps days as a reminder of what it was like to just play — clips of him getting kicked in the shins and then jumping right back up to his feet, clips of him tracking back and fighting to recover lost balls. And he asked Davies about his earliest memories in the game so he could rekindle "that feeling and, more importantly, that passion."

"He was able to talk about those experiences of turning up with no football boots and just falling in love with it," Herdman said of his conversation with Davies that night. "And then I was trying to bring him to that state of mind and that state of emotion about the moment that stood in front of him, which was a chance to start writing a new script for Canada."

They also discussed the role Davies would play against the U.S.

Herdman had devised an unorthodox game plan. Canada would line up in a 4-2-2-2 formation with a four-man midfield shaped in a box. And Davies would start as one of the two forwards up top, as opposed to his usual left wing or back positions, allowing him to play with more attacking freedom.

For years, Canada would sit back against teams like the U.S. and hope for the best. Maybe they could nick a goal on the counter-attack. Maybe they could squeak out a draw.

But Herdman wanted the Canadians to go full throttle.

He wanted to put the Americans under pressure from the first minute until the last.

And he wanted Davies to lead the way from the front.

"I asked the kid to go and press for 90 minutes," Herdman said. "No Canadian team had ever done that against the U.S., to press for 90 minutes. And I said, 'Look, all of that passion, all of those things that you've got inside of you, it's going to come out tomorrow in maybe 90 minutes. It could only be 60 minutes, it could be

50 minutes. But you need to commit to making sure that those Americans feel something different. They can see it. But they've got to feel something different.'

"And that kid, he pressed."

He also scored the game's opening goal, sending the home crowd at Toronto's BMO Field into a frenzy.

Of course, it was him. It had to be him.

In the 63rd minute, Davies beat his defender to the back post to receive a cross from Scott Arfield and almost willed the ball into the goal, falling into the net as the ball just barely crossed the goal line.

He called it the biggest goal of his career.

It certainly wasn't the prettiest, but it was the most meaningful.

Davies said he had a million emotions running through him as he ran to the sidelines and leaped into the air before getting mobbed by his teammates.

Canada finally had its moment.

A few minutes later, Davies was subbed out of the game. He gave everything he had — and then some. So he put on a black jacket and became Canada's biggest cheerleader.

When Lucas Cavallini scored in stoppage time to seal the victory for Canada, Davies sprinted to the end of the field to join him in celebration, grabbing him by the shoulders and screaming at the top of his lungs. And when the final whistle sounded, he was the first player to run onto the field from the sidelines.

"Pulisic came off and sat in the dugout, started to cry, and banged the dugout," Herdman said, referencing USA's star player who was subbed out of the game just a few minutes before Davies. "Davies came off, shook every player's hand, and then was cheering from behind the team.

"You would expect the star player who has scored a goal to come off and start shaking his head and whatever else. He wasn't. He was willing to write that script by putting the effort in that every man was going to put in and then bring his quality, which was to score the goal and terrorize the USA."

As Herdman said in his post-match press conference, the Canadian men's national team had been "hurting for a long time." They'd been waiting for a night like this.

They *needed* one.

"It was a real marker and a historic moment," Herdman said. "Our main motivation, or a huge motivation, is to gain respect. Respect in Canada, then respect in Concacaf, then respect in the world. They really want to be recognized as a football country. And I've said this to the players, we can't talk about it: we have to do it. We have to achieve. Until you achieve results against the USA, Mexico, you won't be seen as the best. You won't be respected."

On that chilly Tuesday night in Toronto, which fell just a day before the seven-year anniversary of Canada's humiliating 8–1 loss in San Pedro Sula, they started to earn some respect. People started to take notice. People started to believe again.

This was "only one little drop in the ocean" of what Herdman wanted for this team, he told reporters. There was still a long way to go — Canada lost 4–1 to the U.S. a month later — but for at least one night, the demons of the past seemed a distant memory.

"Today I saw a different Canada," Cavallini said that night. "A different generation."

A golden one.

In 2014, Canada Soccer held a series of U-15 talent identification camps across the country. It was all part of a "renewed emphasis" to identify the "next generation of high-performance players," as stated in their 2014 Annual Report.

A total of 94 players were scouted that year, including a 13-year-old from the Edmonton Strikers named Alphonso Davies. Interestingly, Davies took part in the identification camp that was geared towards players who were already a part of professional academies.

Davies wasn't.

But he'd caught the attention of the Whitecaps, who then recommended him to Canada Soccer. He was one of just two players there who wasn't already affiliated with one of Canada's professional clubs.

Some of the players from that camp went on to have decent careers. Others fizzled out.

But little did they know, they'd found *the one*.

Davies was selected to represent Canada for the first time the following year. Canada was sending a U-15 team to Mexico City for a prestigious five-nations tournament, in which they'd play friendlies against Qatar, Bermuda, Panama, and host Mexico. It was the first international competition for Canada's 2000-born players. The start of a new cycle.

And Sean Fleming knew Davies needed to be there.

Most of the players were selected based on their showing in the identification camps and a subsequent Canada Soccer showcase. But Fleming, the longtime Canadian youth national team head coach tasked with leading the group, was also familiar with Davies from his club soccer in Edmonton.

Upon the request of Huoseh, he first went to watch Davies play in a game at the Victoria Soccer Club in Northwest Edmonton. After the game, Huoseh asked Fleming what he thought.

"I always guarded my comments because I wanted to make sure that I wasn't saying something that would come back to bite me a little bit," Fleming said.

So he held his tongue.

Until he went back to the parking lot and got into his car, that is.

"I just screamed out like, 'YES!'" Fleming recalled.

Since they were both based in Edmonton, Fleming and Davies travelled to the tournament together. It was August 2015, and Davies was only 14 years old, but Fleming was immediately struck by his maturity. It's one of the reasons why Davies was named captain for a couple of those games.

"He was just a natural," Fleming said. "People just follow him."

Canada won the silver medal in that tournament. After losing 3–1 to Mexico — Davies scored Canada's lone goal — they beat Qatar, Bermuda, and Panama by a combined score of 14–2 in their final three games. And Davies was named a co-MVP with one of the Mexicans.

"I just laughed when I saw that," Fleming said. "They had two trophies made up because they didn't want to just give it to a Canadian in their own tournament. They had to give out two MVPs."

They might as well have given a third.

Davies wasn't the only Canadian who turned heads. He had a partner in crime.

Jonathan David.

"They had such a unique chemistry that I've never seen before," Fleming said.

There were several parallels between the dynamic duo, beyond their birth year and the first four letters of their last names. They were both immigrants who landed in Canada at a young age. Born in the United States to Haitian parents, David moved to Haiti at three months old before settling in Canada at age six.

They were both plucked from their city's local soccer league, rather than a professional academy. At the time, David was a member of Ottawa Gloucester SC.

And best of all?

They both had a knack for the net.

Davies and David were Canada's joint leading scorers in Mexico, each scoring four goals in four games. Fleming played David as an out-and-out centre forward, whereas Davies was used in a few different positions — out wide, as a central attacking midfielder. But it didn't even matter where they played.

They just always seemed to find each other.

"Jonathan would slip it to Alphonso, Alphonso would slip it to Jonathan, and they'd set each other up for these tap-in goals," Fleming recalled. "Normally we would have to really work hard to get goals at the international youth level. I remember talking to one of the staff members and saying, 'I don't remember a time we've had this many tap-ins.' But it was their movement, the way they would find those soft spots, the way they could lose their defenders, it was just incredible."

Even more incredible?

It was the first time they'd ever played together.

Fleming had coached a lot of very good players through his many years with the national team program, including some who went on to have long and fruitful careers at the international level. But when it comes to "individual star quality," Davies and David were in a class of their own.

In the years following that first national team camp in Mexico, they went on different paths. Unlike Davies, who joined the Whitecaps that summer, David bypassed Canada's professional clubs and moved directly to Europe — despite the Whitecaps' best efforts to sign him as well. But they both found their way to the very top.

If this is Canada's golden generation, then Davies and David are the golden boys.

Fittingly, they were both among the finalists for the prestigious Golden Boy award in 2020, recognizing the best young players in Europe aged 21 or younger. Davies had just completed his breakout season with Bayern, while David was the joint leading scorer in Belgium's top tier with KAA Gent.

Some of the previous winners of the award included Wayne Rooney, Lionel Messi, and Kylian Mbappé. To see one Canadian in contention, let alone two, was unheard of. And not only were they in contention. Davies finished 3rd in voting, while David came in at 17th. Regardless, their mere inclusion was a remarkable feat.

These days, David is known as the "Iceman."

He just quietly goes about his business and scores goals.

He burst onto the scene in Europe, scoring five goals in his first five games with Gent. He scored 13 goals in his first season with French club Lille OSC after a Canadian-record 30-million-euro transfer, the most goals ever scored by a Canadian in one of Europe's top five leagues, before breaking his own record the following year. And by age 22, he was already among the top three leading goalscorers in Canadian men's national team history.

"He doesn't really say too much off the pitch," Davies told Canada Soccer after assisting two of David's three goals and scoring the other in a 4–0 World Cup qualifying win over Suriname in June 2021, "but you definitely hear him on the pitch if he wants the ball."

The success Davies and David are having for both club and country is unprecedented. In the context of Canadian soccer, it's hard to talk about one of them without mentioning the other. And if you ask either of them, that's perfectly OK.

"Phonzie is much more outgoing, but they're both humble and they're both very down to earth," Paul Dolan said. "They don't have big heads, they don't think of themselves as being better than anybody else."

"Look at the way they work together, the way they interact with each other," David Edgar added. "Alphonso Davies doesn't want to make it the Alphonso Davies national team. He's just as happy for everyone else to be successful . . . It's frightening what those two could do together."

Just ask the poor kids who tried to defend them all those years ago in Mexico City.

Back then, one of Fleming's priorities as a coach for the Canadian youth national teams was to build a culture. Like a kindergarten teacher can help shape a child's attitude about school, he thought there was an opportunity to do the same with how players felt about representing their country.

He wanted the players to know what that meant.

So he and his staff would have the group sing the Canadian national anthem every morning, for example. They'd have fans and various Canadian soccer legends send in messages for the team. And they'd display a wall of fame highlighting some of the great Canadian men's national team players of the past and sometimes present — an idea that emerged from a conversation Fleming had with Hockey Canada.

"I wanted them to know, who's Bruce Wilson? Who's Dale Mitchell? Who's the best Canadian goalkeeper you think we've had?" Fleming said. "I'd ask them to do research and they'd come up with names."

It's been a while since Fleming has gone through that exercise. In fact, the U-15 tournament in Mexico was his last with Canada Soccer. It was the end of an era. But it was also the start of a new one led by two generational talents who most certainly would be leading candidates for Canada's wall of fame now.

"They're playing at the highest level in the world," Fleming said. "Would it not be natural that Alphonso Davies and Jonathan David would be up there?"

Canada's U-20 national team was going through customs at Heathrow Airport in London, England, when someone noticed that Davies had been pulled into another room.

Davies was 15 years old.

Canada Soccer was working with an immigration lawyer to fast-track his Canadian citizenship application, but it hadn't been processed yet. And there was a mix-up with some travel documentation. So there he was, stuck in a holding room after a long flight, fielding all sorts of questions with the help of Canada's team doctor.

Around 90 minutes went by before he finally emerged.

"Luckily they let him in," said Rob Gale, Canada's U-20 head coach at the time.

Canada Soccer knew they had something in Davies.

Internally, his performances with Canada's U-15s and emergence with the Whitecaps had people talking. So, in March 2016, Gale called him into the U-20 national team for a friendly against England. He was three or four years younger than a lot of players on the team, but they wanted to get him integrated and exposed to these types of environments as early as possible.

"I knew some people at the [English Football Association], and they called me and said 'Look, we're looking for a game on short notice. Would you be interested?" Gale recalled. "So we kind of put it together and I said, 'If we do it, we want to be able to bring in younger players. It won't actually be an Under-20 team.' And they were looking for their team to be slightly older and put in some of the Under-21s who were going to play in the Toulon Tournament later that summer."

So they struck an agreement. England would be a bit older. Canada would be a bit younger.

Or in Davies's case, a lot younger.

The inclusion of Davies, 15, on a U-20 national team roster made a headline or two in Canada. But in England, this game was all about their own teenage prodigy, Marcus Rashford.

Rashford, 18, had taken the country by storm.

Just a month earlier, he scored two goals in his first official game for Manchester United in the UEFA Europa League. Three days later, he scored two more goals and added an assist for good measure in his English Premier League debut against Arsenal. And then, if that wasn't enough, he scored the lone goal in his first-ever Manchester Derby just a week before the game against Canada.

He hadn't yet represented the Three Lions at the senior international level, but suddenly there were calls to include him in their squad for Euro 2016. That would come a few months later. For now, all eyes were on his debut with England's U-20s.

"Literally, it was all the hype," Gale said.

The game would be played in Doncaster, England, on Easter Sunday. Rashford was on the front cover of the matchday program and featured prominently inside.

"They were like, 'This guy always scores on his debuts and now here's his England debut,'" Gale recalled. "So everybody was just coming to see Marcus Rashford dink a few goals on his debut past a Canadian team. Who the heck are they? Nobody expected anything of us."

Aside from themselves.

Gale decided to start both Davies and Ballou Tabla, his two youngest players, right in the middle of the park. If they were going to talk the talk about a new Canadian DNA, a new generation, they figured they might as well walk the walk and let the kids play.

"Let's give them a game," Gale thought.

That's exactly what they did.

Canada won 2–1 off a pair of well-taken goals by Kadin Chung and Marco Bustos. Rashford didn't score, but he did set up England's lone tally.

And Davies, who played 65 minutes, held his own.

"And that takes some personality at a young age," Gale said. "Coming in and playing against these established stars, he easily could have got star-struck by the other team. These recognized Premier League players throughout the squad, the whole fanfare around Marcus Rashford. But he tried to play, he tried to get on the ball, he tried to be energetic, and he didn't shy away from the battle."

The game against England's U-20s kick-started Davies's 2016 campaign, in which he'd really start to make a name for himself in Vancouver. Before long, fans started to call for his inclusion in the Canadian senior men's national team. But there was a cloud of uncertainty around that discussion.

Did Davies have his Canadian citizenship yet? What if he wanted to play for Liberia? Was he eligible to represent Ghana? Too many times had Canada lost promising dual nationals to other countries. There was a fear that might happen again. And ultimately it did with the captain of the U-20 team that Gale took to England, and Davies's roommate on that trip: Fikayo Tomori.

Fortunately for Canada, Davies had a singular focus.

"The one beautiful thing about Alphonso was very early on he stated that he really wanted to play for Canada," Gale said, while acknowledging it was very much a discussion to avoid "the errors of the past."

For his part, Davies said this wasn't much of a question in his mind. He grew up in Canada. He started playing soccer in Canada. It was always going to be Canada.

The biggest hurdle wasn't getting a commitment from Davies.

It was getting his passport.

Without citizenship, Davies couldn't officially play for the men's national team — only in friendlies at the youth level, as was the case in Mexico and England. There was hope that he'd be able to play in the 2017 Concacaf Gold Cup, the marquee event of the region, but the clock was ticking.

"I was monitoring that momentous occasion literally daily, if not hourly, checking in when that was going to take place," then-Canadian men's national team head coach Octavio Zambrano said of Davies's citizenship application. "Because there was obviously a legal process behind it. The moment I was notified that he had become a Canadian citizen, I called him immediately and I obviously congratulated him on becoming a citizen of a great country like Canada. And also to assure him that his time in the national team was going to start immediately. That I wanted him to join the team as fast as possible."

They had him on a flight within 24 hours.

There was some internal debate, but Zambrano saw the 16-year-old as a surefire starter.

After making his debut in a friendly against Curaçao, becoming the youngest player in Canadian men's national team history, Davies was named to Canada's roster for the Gold Cup. By playing in that tournament, he'd officially commit his allegiance and become "cap-tied" to Canada.

"I remember he came into camp and everyone was saying, 'We gotta get this kid capped, he needs to get capped,'" said Russell Teibert, a two-time Canadian U-17 Player of the Year. "Everybody wanted this kid to play for Canada. You could not deny how special he was. We've never had a player like that in Canada in our history."

Teibert roomed with Davies that tournament.

They'd set up the room a bit differently, placing the couch in front of the TV so Davies could play video games. They also watched the entire *Kung Fu Panda* series, because Teibert joked that Davies didn't have the attention span for anything else.

But when it was time to focus, he was able to flip a switch.

"He'd be singing and dancing, and you think, 'You know, Phonzie, we've got a game,'" Teibert recalled. "Then all of a sudden he'd put on his Messi clips and just be glued to the TV, and you know he's in that mindset, he's ready to go."

The night before their first game, Teibert told Davies that he needed to start scoring some goals. It was just a little friendly razzing, because Davies had yet to score for the Whitecaps in MLS despite the hype. But he delivered, bagging two goals in a 4–2 win over French Guiana. After the second one, Teibert grabbed hold of Davies and wrapped his arms around his shoulders in jubilation.

"It's just like, I told you to get one, and he got two," Teibert said in amazement.

He scored in the next game, too, helping Canada earn a 1–1 draw with Costa Rica. By that point, Zambrano said, scouts and agents were literally swarming the lobby at Canada's hotel.

They all wanted time with Canada's new shiny toy.

"We began to kind of monitor the lobby to make sure we wouldn't get unwanted visitors when it was resting time," Zambrano said, adding that they tried to accommodate a couple of short meetings.

Davies was the talk of the tournament.

He won the Golden Boot Award as the leading goalscorer, by virtue of a tiebreaker, and the Young Player Award as the most promising player. He was also named to the tournament's Best XI. It was his coming-out party for Canada.

And as Herdman told reporters in a press conference the following year, it started to "change the mindset" about what this team could be.

Canada lost to Jamaica in the quarterfinals, but it was the first time they'd gone that far since 2009. In the two previous Gold Cups, Canada didn't even score a goal, let alone win a game. Senior players spoke about how Davies gave them new life. New belief.

New hope.

Davies was in tears.

In a matter of days, he was slated to return to BC Place and play for Canada for the first time after his high-profile move to Bayern. His face was plastered over all the posters and billboards. It was supposed to be his homecoming.

But after stretching a ligament in his knee, ironically while celebrating his first goal in the Bundesliga, he was ordered a few days' rest and would be forced to miss the game.

Herdman said Davies was "devastated" when they spoke on the phone. He could barely finish his sentences. At one point, someone had to grab the phone from him and finish the call.

"This meant a lot to him," Herdman said at the time.

He didn't want to let his country down.

But here's the beauty of it: he didn't. With Davies watching from a suite above — he decided to make the trip anyway, even though he couldn't play — Canada won the game 4–1. The opponent was French Guiana, so they should have been expected to win regardless. But there was something symbolic about Canada coming through without their ringer.

"I think we've got the talent here for someone to really step through and start to show Canada that there's more to this team than Alphonso Davies," Herdman said that week.

That became evident at the 2021 Concacaf Gold Cup.

Neither Davies nor David participated in the tournament due to injuries and the start of their respective club campaigns in Europe. Cyle Larin, one of Canada's most prolific strikers, also suffered an injury in the group stage. Canada was missing several key contributors.

And yet they went toe to toe with both the U.S. and Mexico, beat Costa Rica handily, and reached the semifinals for the first time since 2007. Other players, like the tournament's breakout star, Tajon Buchanan, stepped up and staked their claim.

They never had that luxury in the past.

Nowadays, there are Canadian players littered across Europe. They're everywhere. In 2021 alone, there were at least seven Canadian men's players who were a part of championship-winning teams in their respective European competitions.

Closer to home, there are more Canadian players getting minutes in MLS than ever before. And Canada finally has its own domestic league, the Canadian Premier League, which has long been seen as the missing piece for the development of young Canadian players.

All the stars appear to be aligning.

Not to mention, highly touted dual nationals are actually *choosing* to play for Canada. Like striker Iké Ugbo, who opted to represent Canada despite being eligible to play for both Nigeria and England, and Stephen Eustáquio, a standout midfielder who'd previously been a part of Portugal's youth national team system.

When Herdman first took over the Canadian men's national team in 2018, he said it was a "tough conversation" when trying to recruit players.

Not anymore.

"People can genuinely see the talent in the squad with Alphonso," he said. "More importantly, they want to play with him. That's what you can say, 'These generations come around once every 10, 15, 20 years. You can be part of that generation.' And that generation typically needs a generational leader. That's Alphonso. For me, it's being able to say to a young kid, 'In the next 10 years, you could be playing with one of the best 11 players in the world.'"

Herdman likened Davies to Gareth Bale of Wales. Wales had other elite talents when they reached the semifinals of Euro 2016, their first major competition in 58 years. Namely, Aaron Ramsey. One player alone will not lead any team to glory. It takes an army.

But Bale was the centrepiece for Wales. And Davies is for Canada.

For a while, there was just one missing piece.

And it's the same one that Herdman saw with Christine Sinclair when he first started working with her in 2011. Sinclair is the greatest Canadian soccer player of all time.

Hands down. No questions asked. End of debate.

But her legacy wasn't truly cemented until she scored a hat-trick against the U.S. at the 2012 Olympics and put a bronze medal around her neck. That's when she changed the sport forever. When Canada won an Olympic gold medal nine years later, there were players on that team who chose to pursue a career in the game because of what they saw from Sinclair and the Canadian women's national team in 2012.

"When you win something or when you do something that's unexpected, that's the moment where you go from being known and respected to being revered," said Herdman, who coached the Canadian women for seven years before a controversial move to the men's team. "And you shift into that legendary category. I think Sinc's hat-trick at the Olympic Games was the moment for her."

Herdman knew Davies's moment had to be on the biggest stage, when Canada is seen as an underdog, and the whole country is watching. It had to be at a World Cup.

But first, they had to get there.

CHAPTER 15:
WORLD CUP DREAMS

They were so close, yet so far.

For the first time in more than two decades, Canada's men's national team was competing in the final round of World Cup qualifying: the Octagonal, an evolution from the Hexagonal of years past. The format was slightly different due to the pandemic — there were eight teams rather than six — but the path remained the same. Play each team twice, finish in the top three of the standings, and guarantee your place at the World Cup.

This was Canada's sixth game. Although they were undefeated in the first five, they only had a single win under their belt. The rest were draws.

And they knew that wasn't going to cut it.

"If there's any game we've got to win to really set the tone, it's this one," John Herdman told reporters on the eve of their October 13, 2021 encounter with Panama at BMO Field.

Canada came into the game one point back of Panama for the third and final automatic World Cup berth in the Concacaf region. If they were to draw again or, worse, lose outright, qualifying for Qatar 2022 would become an even taller task.

"Deep down, we felt a lot of pressure there," said Canadian defender Alistair Johnston.

Imagine, then, the feeling when Panama opened the scoring less than five minutes into the game, with thousands of fans still trickling into the stadium.

Now, the pressure was *really* on.

"Those are the kinds of games you need your big-time players to show up," Johnston added.

Enter Davies.

Starting alongside Jonathan David in a two-striker system, much like he did against the U.S. on that same field almost two years ago to the day, Davies put the team on his back.

Twice in the 10 minutes following Panama's goal, he set up David for point-blank opportunities, including a dazzling dribbling display in which he weaved through a maze of five Panamanian players before slipping a short pass into David at the top of the box. He was at it again shortly later, this time going for goal himself with a powerful long-range strike after dancing past a few more Panamanian defenders.

"He took on four or five players and got a shot off and the stadium kind of woke up," said defender Kamal Miller. "From then, we flipped a switch."

It felt like an equalizer was coming. Davies was going to make sure of it.

Just before the half-hour mark, he delivered an in-swinging corner kick that ricocheted into the net off the shoulder of a Panamanian defender.

Game on.

The score remained 1–1 heading into the second half, despite continued pressure from Canada. Eventually, they started to lose momentum. There was a period just before the 60th minute when Panama controlled the ball for the entirety of a three-and-a-half-minute stretch.

"They were just switching it side to side, and it seemed like we couldn't really get close to the ball," Miller said.

Something needed to change.

Herdman even considered subbing Davies off, feeling he was running out of gas. But instead he moved Davies to the right wing from his forward position, made a couple other substitutions as well as a formation change, and called the team onto the sideline to provide further instruction — conveniently made possible thanks to what appeared to be a "tactical injury" for Canadian goalkeeper Maxime Crépeau, designed to pause the game.

"Listen in, listen in, listen in," Herdman shouted as the group gathered around.

His main message was to get Canada's back line higher and more connected with the rest of the team. He certainly couldn't have drawn up what happened next.

No one could have.

Less than one minute after play resumed, Canada won possession of the ball near the top of their 18-yard box. A short pass was then played to David, who quickly turned and punted a hopeful long ball down the right wing assuming Davies was there. He wasn't. Not even close.

Until he was.

"For some reason, Phonzie starts sprinting," Johnston recalled. "And I was kind of looking up ahead like, 'What's he seeing that I'm not seeing?' Because for me, it was such an open-shut case. The centre back was either going to take possession and play forward or just let it roll out of play . . . But you saw him sprinting and you could sense that his Spidey senses were going. He smelled a little bit of a blood in the water. And he kicked it into that top gear."

"I had no idea what he was thinking," Miller added. "I thought he was chasing the ball down so he could just go in and smash the guy, like I thought he was a bit frustrated. I thought he was going to take a yellow on that play. But I was very wrong."

Davies picked up steam as the ball trickled towards the sideline, seemingly headed out of bounds. Eventually realizing Davies was rapidly approaching, the Panamanian defender tried to beat him to the line and shield the ball out of play. But it was too late.

At that point, there was no stopping him.

"It was like a cheetah chasing a gazelle," Herdman would later tell TSN *OverDrive*.

In one magnificent motion, Davies jumped around the defender, contorted his body, and dragged the ball off the line with the top of his trailing right foot.

All while going full speed.

"It was just such an unbelievable half a second of body control and balance," Johnston said. "As soon as he got by that guy, we completely stopped. The crowd as well, as he got closer and closer to that play, you could just sense them all standing up on that side. You just knew something was happening. Boom, he does that. And instantly we're all spectators. As much as our coaching staff would hate to say it . . . we all stopped and just held our breath. It just felt like one of those moments. And it ended up being that."

Now in full control, Davies attacked the Panamanian box with only one defender to beat. He also had Tajon Buchanan available to his left. But he finished what he started, cutting inside onto his left foot, taking a step back to give himself some space, and firing a low, off-balance strike past the sliding defender and into the bottom right corner of the goal. The goalkeeper froze, expecting Davies to shoot towards the largely vacated far post. It would have been the logical move, with all his momentum carrying him in that direction.

But in many ways, this play was devoid of logic.

"I was in shock because everything I saw happening on the play was the opposite of what I thought was going to happen," Miller said. "I thought he was going to get a yellow card first of all, and then he won the ball. Then I thought he was going to pass to Tajon, and then he took it himself. And I thought he was going to cut in and shoot to the far post, and then he cut it back to the first post. I really just couldn't believe it."

Neither could fellow defender Sam Adekugbe, who had just subbed into the game.

"When he scored, I was literally like, 'What the fuck?'" Adekugbe recalled. "BMO went crazy. BMO went, like, *crazy* . . . I'm not even talking about the loudness of the stadium, but the *electricity*. Just the energy is like something you can't really explain, you know what I mean? It was like a lightning bolt just struck through the stadium."

In more ways than one.

Davies reached a blazing fast top speed of 37.1 km/h while chasing down the ball, as per Canada Soccer, and covered 80 yards in total — more than two-thirds the length of the field.

"That was the most athletic play I've ever seen live, whether being on the field or watching something in person in the crowd,"

Johnston said. "It was honestly one of the most mesmerizing things."

There aren't many players in the world who would have been able to do what Davies did in those 13 seconds, not only catching up to and corralling the loose ball but also having the skill and poise to finish the play. There are probably even fewer players who would have bothered trying. Especially considering this was his third game in a week with the national team, having just played the full 90 minutes in both Mexico and Jamaica.

Somehow, someway, he found it within himself.

"He really wants this," Herdman said after the game, which Canada ended up winning 4–1. "He's dreaming of taking this country to a World Cup."

Unbeknownst to much of the country, Canada began their World Cup qualifying campaign about seven months earlier, in March 2021.

Since they weren't among the top five ranked teams in Concacaf, they had to start in the first round and play minnows like Bermuda, the Cayman Islands, Aruba, and Suriname. Due to pandemic restrictions, all those games were hosted at neutral and mostly empty stadiums in the U.S. It was *far* from glamorous. And yet, even back then, Herdman started to realize how much this meant to his young superstar.

Canada's second game of the campaign was against the Cayman Islands. They didn't just want to win. They wanted to be "ruthless." With one little slip-up, they knew their World Cup dreams could be over before they even started. And they certainly didn't want to leave anything to chance. So prior to the game, they set a target of scoring at least nine goals, which would be a new team record. Herdman tasked midfielder David Wotherspoon with grabbing the ball from the back of the net after each Canadian goal and bringing it to centre field so they could quickly restart play and go for another one.

The first half went as planned, with Canada leading 6–0 at the break. But they started a little slow in the second half, going nearly 20 minutes without a goal.

"You go into that comfort zone," Herdman said. "It's just going to happen."

When they finally scored their seventh, it wasn't Wotherspoon who went to get the ball. It wasn't the goalscorer, either. Out of the corner of his eye, Herdman noticed it was Davies.

"When you think about that, and you put it into perspective, here he is playing at IMG, which is an amateur, semi-professional stadium with maybe 500 seats and a half a stand," Herdman said. "He's playing against an amateur team of taxi drivers, butchers, and newsagents. We're 6–0 up, just scored the seventh, and here's a guy who's earning, I don't know what he's earning, he's just won every trophy to be won, and there he is picking the ball out of the back of the net and returning it back to the field."

"It tells us something," Herdman continued. "He wants this country to qualify for a World Cup. It's serious for him. He's a funny guy, he expresses himself on the pitch, and he has that other side to him, but this guy is a ruthless competitor as well. And I don't want anyone not to see that . . . That moment was just a reminder to me that you're dealing with a real competitor here. A guy who is clear he's going to bring this team to a World Cup."

Canada won the game 11–0. Fittingly, Davies scored the record-breaking ninth goal.

"You said you were going to be ruthless, and you fucking lived that identity," Herdman told the team post-game, as seen in Canada Soccer's #WeCAN documentary series.

As World Cup qualifying went on, and the stakes got a little higher, Davies began to exert his influence on the group even further.

In the days leading up to their first game of the Octagonal, the team gathered in a third-floor meeting room at the Delta Hotel in downtown Toronto. These introductory meetings were held at the start of every camp, where Herdman would have a PowerPoint presentation set up and lay out what he called the "missions" for their upcoming games.

"The whole team's there, the room goes dark, and John goes into one of his famous speeches that gets all the guys just absolutely fired up," Johnston explained.

In this particular meeting, Herdman outlined some of the historical point totals typically required from the final round to qualify for the World Cup. Then he started mapping out Canada's entire 14-match schedule. The mission, as he laid out, was to win every single game at home and go undefeated on the road.

Is that all, coach?

"Right when that slide went up, I was kind of expecting there to be a bit more of a gasp, like, 'Oh my gosh, does he really expect us to do that?'" Johnston recalled.

But it was the opposite. There was an air of confidence in the room. As Adekugbe recalled, the discussion eventually came to "What games can we win away from home?"

Davies wasn't usually outspoken in these settings. He left the talking to the senior players on the team. But in that moment, he spoke up and said, "All of them."

"I'll never forget that meeting," Miller said. "To hear that from him, I had goosebumps."

Realistically, what Davies was suggesting was close to impossible. It just didn't happen. And ultimately it wouldn't for Canada, either. But the fact that it was even spoken, and they *believed* it was possible, was all that really mattered.

"He's shaping the mentality of this new Canada," Herdman concluded.

That was evident in Canada's first two away games of the Octagonal, in which he assisted the game-tying goals in historic 1–1 draws against the U.S. and Mexico — the two traditional giants of the region. And it was certainly evident that October night against Panama.

If you ask Miller, that was the night Davies "took a big step" towards cementing his role as a leader on the team. Considering his age, Miller said, it's not necessarily a role they expect from him. And yet he still finds a way to "compose the team, especially in tough moments."

"In big games," Miller added, "you always hear his voice."

The Panama game was a prime example.

Early on, when a snake-bitten David passed up a point-blank opportunity, Davies reminded him that he was a "natural striker" and that his job was to score goals.

"Next time you have the shot, shoot it," Davies told him.

And that's exactly what David did when he found himself in a similar position shortly later. The goalkeeper saved it, but Davies put his arms around David, patted him on the back, and encouraged him to keep going. He'd score a goal later in the game.

Then there was the moment just before halftime, when Davies came to the defence of his teammates during a bench-clearing melee near the corner flag. Or right after the final whistle, when he helped calm teammate Richie Laryea to prevent another altercation.

Once cooler heads prevailed, Canada huddled at centre field as per usual. After veteran Steven Vitória said a few words, someone pushed Davies into the middle of the circle.

"It was his moment," Johnston said. "It had to be."

"I just want to say," Davies commenced as seen in the #WeCAN documentary series, before everyone interjected with cheers and laughter.

He went on to say that he was "devastated" to miss the game against El Salvador a month earlier and how happy he was to be there with the team in that moment.

"Good three points," he concluded. "Let's keep going in November!"

More cheers and laughter ensued.

"You could just see the smiles and the relief," Johnston recalled. "To end a window like that with such a massive win, it just filled us with such confidence. And he was the guy that did it. He was the guy that spearheaded that performance. You could also just see the relief for him. He's under so much pressure. People don't understand that, either. He's been the face of Canada Soccer for now the past five years, since he was 16 years old. He's felt that burden of taking this country to that next level. And that was a really big moment for him . . . I think that kind of felt like getting the monkey off his back to a degree in that World Cup qualification campaign, that he really felt that 'OK, you know what, it is true, I am the best player in Concacaf.' It's something that we all knew, and deep down, I think he knew too. But to have a moment like that . . . I think that really instilled him with a lot of confidence that he is the leader of this team. He is the best player. He could be the one that could take us there."

In his post-game press conference, Herdman was asked about Davies's evolution as a leader. And he offered perhaps the best compliment anyone could ask for.

"It reminds us of Sinclair," Herdman said. "When he speaks, people listen."

In the same press conference, Herdman revealed that Drake had reached out to Davies wanting to meet up after the game, which quickly made the rounds on social media. Meanwhile, Johnston had just picked up his phone in the locker room and opened Twitter.

It was the first thing he saw.

"Alphonso was straight across the locker room from me, all of 10 feet away, and I went, 'Phonzie, did Drake text you?'" Johnston recalled.

"What? Did he?" he remembered Davies saying.

"I don't know, check your phone, look at this tweet," Johnston responded.

"So he pulled out his phone, he's flying through his DMs, obviously it's Alphonso Davies, a bit more Instagram requests and messages than I've ever seen, he's flying through them and he can't find it. He's like, 'Oh no no no, did I miss Drake's text?' He couldn't believe it."

As it turns out, Drake had reached out to a member of Canada's medical staff — not Davies himself — to request the meet-up. Regardless, Johnston said there was "pandemonium" as word travelled around the locker room.

"My phone was getting passed around, everyone was seeing the tweet and realizing, 'Oh my gosh, Drake wants to meet us. Does this mean we finally made it to that level where we're mainstream now?'"

That's exactly what it meant.

The highlight of Davies's end-to-end goal had gone viral. The front page of TSN.ca was all Canada and all Davies, which is especially notable considering the Toronto Maple Leafs had opened their NHL season the same evening. It was the talk of the nation. A watershed moment. And perhaps the greatest goal ever scored in the history of the national team.

"I've watched that Davies goal about 30 times," prominent *TSN Hockey* host James Duthie tweeted. "It's incredible."

Finally, *finally*, it felt like the Canadian men's national team had made it.

When they got back to the hotel, a blacked-out Escalade was waiting to pick up Davies and a couple others — to his disappointment, he was told everyone couldn't come — and bring them to meet Drake at a nearby Italian restaurant called Sotto Sotto.

"I said, 'OK, yeah, we're getting there,'" Johnston chuckled. "Slowly but surely."

Herdman is known as a master motivator.

Leading up to the 2012 Olympic Games, he showed the Canadian women's national team a photo of a dejected Christine Sinclair sitting on the field with a broken nose and tears running down her face following their disappointing exit from the 2011 Women's World Cup.

Then he asked the players what they saw.

"We've been letting you down for 10 years," one of them told her. "Not this time."

That day, they promised Sinclair they'd make her cry again. And when Canada won a bronze medal at those Olympics, she did. Herdman helped instill a greater purpose within the locker room. A deeper connection. And he tried to do the same when he took over the men's team in 2018. He talked about being pioneers. Leaving a legacy. Bringing the country together.

After beating Panama the way they did, all those things started to feel possible.

In their next two games, they drew enormous crowds of 48,806 and 44,212 on a couple frigid and snowy November nights in Edmonton — the first time Davies had played there since leaving home at age 14. Canada won both of them, beating Costa Rica and Mexico to jump into first place. Prime Minister Justin Trudeau popped in for a visit that trip, addressing the team inside the Commonwealth Fieldhouse, where Davies used to train. Wayne Gretzky sent a video message to the team. And broadcast numbers skyrocketed on Canadian television, with more viewers tuning in for those two games than Canada's first six games combined.

"I always just thought John was trying to motivate us," Adekugbe said. "But, for example, when you go to Edmonton and you see 50,000 people, you come to Toronto again and you start to see that more fans are getting there early . . . that all started with the Panama game, you know? There was low-key a lot of Panamanian fans in the stands. We weren't really too happy about that, but after that game, I definitely think the nation started to believe in us."

They also started to believe in themselves.

"Now we could stop thinking about 'Are we good enough to be in this Octagonal?' To now start thinking about 'Alright, what's it going to take to get a guaranteed spot in this World Cup qualification?'" Johnston said. "It really all started with that goal."

"That kind of turned the tide of our whole qualifying," Miller agreed.

Davies did that.

But little did anyone know at the time, he wasn't going to be able to see it through to the finish line. After returning from his winter holidays, Davies was one of several Bayern Munich players who tested positive for COVID-19 in the first week of January 2022. So he had to self-isolate. A week later, he was back on the training field and feeling good. But then, as he was sitting at home about to play *FIFA*, he got a call from the team doctor.

"There's something going on with your heart," the doctor told him, as Davies recounted to ESPN's Archie Rhind-Tutt.

On January 14, 2022, Bayern Munich revealed that Davies would be sidelined until further notice with an inflammation of the heart muscle. Bayern's medical staff detected the condition, known as myocarditis, in a standard follow-up exam after Davies's bout with COVID, though doctors couldn't determine the cause with certainty.

"It doesn't matter if Alphonso Davies had this from the flu, from Omicron, Delta, or whatever," Bayern head coach Julian Nagelsmann told reporters. "That's not really the decisive factor. The situation is that it's absolutely awful, terrible. What can I say?"

Nagelsmann described it is as a "mild" case of myocarditis. And

Davies wasn't showing any symptoms. But there was still great uncertainty as to when he'd return to full health.

"The first thing that came to my mind was 'Oh my god, this guy can't play soccer again,'" Adekugbe recalled. "Done at 22, 21, no way, this can't be true."

Adekugbe said he and Davies spoke on the phone for half an hour before the news came out, and before Davies had spoken to his parents. Davies told him that it was a small inflammation, and the club was being overly careful.

"He was, like, *devastated*, but he wasn't worried," Adekugbe said. "So, when he wasn't worried, I wasn't worried."

Still, Davies called it the lowest point of his career. His biggest frustration was the unknown timeline and the fact that he had to stop all physical activities to keep his heart rate down.

"I don't know, it's just, I couldn't do anything," he told ESPN. "I couldn't even work out. I was just a couch potato."

During that time, Davies's parents came to visit him in Munich. And Adekugbe, one of his closest friends on the national team, would usually call to check in once a week. Those things helped, of course, but as time went on, his mind started to wander into a dark place.

"I would just go for scans every few weeks and it was tough because I felt my career could have ended," Davies said. "I just didn't know what was going on with it at the time. It was a scary moment for me."

Initially, Davies thought he might only be out for three weeks. After his first check-up, he was told things were heading in the right direction, which had everyone feeling optimistic.

"For me, it was goosebumps," Bayern technical director Marco Neppe recalled.

But then three weeks became three months, which, coincidentally, was around the same amount of time Canada had remaining in World Cup qualifying. There was a glimmer of hope that Davies could maybe recover — or at least join the group — in time for the final few games, but Bayern's medical staff deemed that it was a bit too soon.

If Canada was going to qualify, they'd have to do it without him.

"Me personally, I was devastated," Miller said. "Not only for the team, but for the country, and most importantly for him."

"I think that was the biggest thing for us," Johnston agreed. "We all just felt heartbroken for him that he was missing out on a lot of those moments, because he deserved to be there. He'd been such an integral part. If there's anyone, *anyone*, who deserved to reap the rewards of what we'd been able to accomplish as a group, it was him."

Up until that point, Davies had played 13 of Canada's 14 games during World Cup qualifying. And he'd directly contributed to 13 goals, recording five goals and eight assists.

Despite missing the final six games, and being on the other side of the globe, he continued to make sure his presence was felt in different ways. Before every game, for example, he'd send the team a good luck message or video in the group chat.

"Not just a regular good luck video," Miller said. "He really went into detail, gave us some good laughs, and kept in contact with everyone on the team."

And whenever the team was together, he'd call Adekugbe on FaceTime or Snapchat and then Adekugbe would pass the phone around to everyone else so they could catch up.

"Whenever you'd see Sam, it wasn't uncommon for Phonzie to be on FaceTime, hanging around with the boys," Miller continued. "We'd be playing Uno and he was there on FaceTime."

He also showed his support for the team publicly, streaming himself watching Canada's games live on Twitch from his Munich home — sometimes into the middle of the night. He was always decked out in Canada gear, rotating between their red, white, and black jerseys. And he couldn't contain his excitement whenever Canada scored, often screaming at the very top of his lungs, jumping around the room, and mimicking the goalscorer's celebration.

"Go, ohhhh, ohhhh, Sammy!" he yelled while bouncing on his seat and grabbing his dad's arm, as Adekugbe broke in on goal late in a game against the U.S.

"Ahhhhhh!" he continued after Adekugbe scored, sealing the victory. "Golazo! Sammyyyy! Come on! Come on! Come on! Woo! Finished! It's over! It's over! It's over!"

So much for keeping that heart rate down.

Adekugbe's phone blew up after the game, with Davies's reaction to his goal going viral.

"I was so happy that he was so happy for me," Adekugbe said. "When your best player on your team has that passion for the country and for his national team, it's so telling about the player but it also brings other players in closer."

"The Twitch streams always had everyone doubled over laughing," Johnston added. "After a game, we'd go and see his highlights and you can just see how much it means to him, the emotions, and also for me, just the funny stuff. When someone would make a mistake, he'd go, 'Oh no, what are you doing here, Sammy?' or something like that."

"It was hilarious," Miller said. "It was a joy to watch. I had some good laughs. But just to see the raw emotion and how much he loves the team and loves Canada is special. Especially from such a big player . . . it doesn't get bigger than Bayern, so the fact that he'd still get up and get excited for these games, especially when he's not a part of them, just shows how much he loves the guys and wants the country to succeed."

And succeed they did.

On March 27, 2022, Canada beat Jamaica 4–0 at BMO Field to officially qualify for the 2022 FIFA World Cup in Qatar, ending the men's national team's 36-year drought. Once again streaming live on Twitch, Davies broke down in tears at the final whistle and fell to the floor.

"You don't understand how long it's been," he said, gesturing to the camera, with tears still running down his face. "You guys don't understand how many times I've heard 'You guys aren't going to make it, you're never going to make it.' We made it, man. Every single person on that pitch deserves this. Every single person in those stands, every single person in Canada, even outside of Canada, that believed in us, this is for you guys."

And if you ask anyone in that locker room, many of whom celebrated with Davies on FaceTime after the game, they'll tell you the same thing: this was for him too.

CHAPTER 16:
THE DAVIES EFFECT

"**P**honzie! Phonzie! Phonzie!"

The chants of his nickname reverberated across the stadium and around the world.

In Buduburam, they were heard in a little viewing centre across from DA Park, the dirt soccer field that Davies once kicked a ball around as a child. These "DSTV Centres," as they're called in Ghana, have a couple of TV sets installed where world soccer games are shown for a fee.

Whenever there's a big game on, this is where people gather.

It's within these centres that many watched Davies announce himself to the world with his breathtaking display against Chelsea in the UEFA Champions League back in February 2020.

You know the one.

"After that game, he was trending in Ghana," said Emmanuel Ayamga, a sportswriter for popular online news platform *Pulse Ghana*. "Some were confused as to whether he was a Ghanaian or a Liberian. So I started reading extensively about him."

After some delays due to the COVID-19 pandemic, and an initial site visit to get a lay of the land, Ayamga decided to make a trip out to Buduburam from nearby Accra in the fall of 2020 to learn more about Davies and the soccer culture at the camp.

Buduburam wasn't what it used to be, he found.

Though known locally as "Liberia Camp," based on its original mandate of housing Liberian refugees, there were people from all over West Africa living there. Liberians. Ghanaians. Togolese. Beninese. Ivorians. Cameroonians. Nigerians.

It wasn't considered an official refugee camp. The UNHCR was no longer present. And according to Ayamga, it had essentially been "cut off" from Ghana as well.

"There was no supervision," Ayamga said. "It was like a survival of the fittest."

Rightly or wrongly, Ayamga said, Buduburam had earned the reputation of being a "rowdy place" that housed all sorts of criminals. There were calls — and since then concrete plans — to demolish the camp altogether and rebuild the area.

But one thing hadn't changed: the passion the people of Buduburam had for soccer.

"If you've followed Ghanaian football for the past decade, in the last five or six years, Ghana football has waned a bit because the national team is not doing as well as they used to," Ayamga said. "So the passion has dropped a bit. But then in Buduburam, the passion was so huge. I was really surprised when I got there and realized almost everybody there was into football."

Because in Buduburam, it wasn't just a game. It was an escape from the harsh realities that surrounded them. It was a lifeline. For some, it was an opportunity to become something in life.

Sadly, the coaches and players Ayamga spoke to on the camp all felt that opportunity was lacking. Buduburam was home to several boys' teams from U-10 to U-18, a women's team, and even professional teams competing in Ghana's Division Two and Division Three.

But without proper financing, facilities, and high-level coaching, they could only go so far. Volunteer coaches typically paid for everything out of their own pockets. Sometimes, they were even asked to provide and care for the kids on their team, which they did out of "true benevolence," as Ayamga put it.

Even the highest-level players weren't compensated, so many of them had to work as masons, carpenters, plumbers, and painters to earn a living. Naturally, these jobs often conflicted with, and took precedence over, their soccer commitments.

"They were playing for the clubs out of passion with the hope that maybe one day their talent will shine bright for some agents to pick them up and help them to progress in their careers," Ayamga said.

All this was the basis of Ayamga's feature article, "It's your talent and Inshallah: The uncertainty of football in the Buduburam refugee camp," which placed fifth in Africa for Best Colour Piece in the writing category at the 2020 International Sports Press Association (AIPS) Sport Media Awards.

"That was one of the quotes from one of the coaches," Ayamga said. "What he was saying, 'It's your talent and Inshallah,' was in terms of raw talent you can find tons of kids on the streets of Buduburam who are as talented as anybody around the world. But when it comes to the support, to get them to mature and develop into professional footballers, it's just by the grace of God. Inshallah means 'by the grace of God.' The real situation on the ground is that your talent alone in Buduburam can't take you far. You need the grace of God as well, like it happened with Alphonso Davies."

Everyone Ayamga spoke to in Buduburam was aware of Davies. And not only aware of him. They "worshipped" him.

"There's a line in my article where I said if Buduburam was a country on its own, Alphonso Davies would be its global ambassador," Ayamga said.

Ayamga learned that the clubs sometimes played exhibition matches on the camp wearing Bayern Munich jerseys. One team wore their home jersey. The other wore their away jersey. And they all had Davies's name on the back.

Growing up, it's common for youngsters to choose a player they pretend to be on the field, or someone they try to model their game after. This happens all over the world, whether they're playing in their backyard, at the school field with their friends, or between houses on a refugee camp. More often than not, they choose Messi or Ronaldo. Maybe Neymar.

Not in Buduburam.

"Almost every kid wanted to be a left back," Ayamga said. "One of the coaches actually told me, he was joking, but he said something like he needs strikers, but everybody wants to be a left back. The kids actually cherish Alphonso Davies."

Despite all their hardships, Davies has given them hope. It was a long time ago, and the circumstances aren't the same. But if he made it, maybe they can too.

Inshallah.

"He's the biggest inspiration for them," Ayamga added. "One of the reasons these guys are not giving up is the fact that they know that one person from their community has been able to rise to the top.

"They see him as a shining light."

Davies was back in town for the first time after his move to Bayern Munich.

His season had just ended. And he was off to join the national team in a few days. But on this Friday night, he was going to be attending a BTB Soccer Academy youth training session at the Clareview Rec Centre, a few blocks from his childhood home in Northeast Edmonton.

So Talal Al-Awaid, co-owner of the academy and one of his old coaches, went to the soccer store to grab some merchandise for Davies to sign. He figured they could use it for an auction or a giveaway. When he got there, Al-Awaid was surprised to hear they didn't have any Bayern Munich jerseys.

Not even one.

"The lady that was working at the store said they sold out that day," Al-Awaid said.

Yes, a soccer store in Edmonton sold out of Bayern Munich jerseys. It all made sense when Al-Awaid made his way to Clareview and saw the crowd of kids eager to meet their hero.

"I don't think I'd ever seen that many Bayern Munich jerseys in a place at once," he said.

Until a couple of years later, of course, when Edmonton's Commonwealth Stadium drew close to 100,000 fans for Davies's homecoming games with the national team.

That's an example of how things have changed.

As John Herdman said in 2018, "There's a new fan base that's built on the back of Alphonso Davies." And that was *before* he ever played a game with Bayern or scored *the goal* against Panama, helping lead Canada back to a World Cup.

He didn't do it alone — Christine Sinclair and the Canadian women's national team deserve as much credit as anyone. And it certainly didn't happen overnight, but Davies has helped put soccer on the map in this hockey-crazed country.

"He's turned a lot of people who would have never gotten into soccer or never followed it into soccer fans or players," Al-Awaid said. "It's the start of building that real soccer culture that's been missing from Canada for a long time. He kind of lit that fuse."

Davies signed autographs, posed for photos, and even trained with the team that night at Clareview. It was the same field he'd trained on countless times before growing up. A lot of the kids in the BTB Academy are from the same part of town as Davies — his younger brother was in the program too. They're using the same facilities as he did. Working with the same coaches. Playing on the same teams. And a lot of them are immigrants who come from similar backgrounds to Davies's. In Davies, they can see a little bit of themselves.

That matters.

"To them, that's their hero," Al-Awaid said. "That's who they look up to. I can only imagine if I got to play with my favourite athlete when I was 10 or 11. That in itself, taking the time to even sit down with them, have a conversation, he'll pick up the little kids, carry them, run around, and do that type of stuff, you wouldn't think this guy's a world-class player playing at the highest level. You'd just think it's one of the coaches on staff helping out."

"He comes home every summer and his presence alone drives these kids to get better," added Jeff Paulus, the former FC Edmonton academy director who's now working at the grassroots level. "Now kids are doing the extra training on their own time, because that's what Alphonso did. Not to say everyone can be Alphonso Davies. He's generational in our country."

When Davies was growing up, he said, he felt like "no one gave Canadians a chance." Although his rise to soccer stardom may never be replicated, he's shown that it's possible. A kid from Canada, from snowy Edmonton, can have a future in the game. Maybe they'll go to college. Maybe they'll play in the Canadian Premier League or Major League Soccer.

Or maybe, just maybe, they'll make it to the top.

"I think the main thing is, he's given everyone hope," said Kassim Khimji, a longtime youth soccer coach in Edmonton. "People see that, hey, a kid that trained at Clareview is playing for Bayern Munich, a kid from Northside Edmonton is a Champions League winner. They never had that before. Before, they would just have a hopeless dream."

Now, that dream doesn't seem so crazy.

That's certainly the feeling over at St. Nicholas, where Davies played his school soccer in junior high. And if the students ever forget, they just have to look up at the giant poster of Davies blown up in the gymnasium, his various accomplishments displayed on the soccer academy wall, or his framed jerseys mounted on the wall in Marco Bossio's classroom.

"It's a constant reminder and a symbol that you can pursue your dreams," Bossio said. "If you put your mind to it, anything is possible. He's living proof."

The impact Davies has made is tangible.

Over at the Whitecaps academy in Vancouver, there's a constant stream of players joining the program from Edmonton every year, pointing to Davies as their inspiration. In the fall of 2022, six players were selected from BTB alone.

More and more young Edmontonians are also getting looks abroad.

Like Muslim Umar, who was selected to represent Bayern Munich's new international youth "world squad" in both of its first two years of existence. He wore number 19, just like Davies. Or Dieu-Merci Michel, who had trials at Bayern and top-division Belgian side, Club Brugge, before joining a team in Portugal.

Both of them were members of the BTB Academy. They were working with the same people that Davies did, including Al-Awaid and Huoseh, who helped facilitate the opportunities. Without Davies, that pathway wouldn't exist. He's a trailblazer.

And not only for Edmontonians.

"When I worked at Chelsea and I took Christian Pulisic there, the reaction was 'An American kid?'" Jorge Alvial recalled. "I mean, they even got mad at me, to be honest. The perception was, from the whole of Europe I would say, that Americans play American football, they play basketball, they play baseball."

And Canadians, of course, play hockey.

"They could never think that an Alphonso Davies or a Christian Pulisic could get to the level that they have," he continued. "Alphonso Davies has won everything that he touched at Bayern Munich. He can change how the world thinks about North America when it comes to football."

In many ways, he already has. That goes for the European clubs, who are shopping around North America more than ever before. And it also goes for how the game is viewed within the continent itself.

"The game is popular again, it's funky again, people want to see him play," Craig Dalrymple said.

After leaving his post as Whitecaps academy director, Dalrymple spent some time working at the grassroots level in the Vancouver area. And all anyone ever wanted to talk about was Davies.

"He's kind of like the Tiger Woods, a little bit, of the sport," Dalrymple said. "He's just this phenom."

In hockey, Canada has had phenoms like Wayne Gretzky, Sidney Crosby, Connor McDavid, Hayley Wickenheiser, and Marie-Philip Poulin, among others. In basketball, Steve Nash was the first to truly reach that level. In soccer, it's always been Sinclair. These are players, people, who have transcended their sports and inspired new generations of fans and athletes. A Canadian men's soccer player had never had such an effect.

Until now.

"There's been many a talented footballer, there's been many an athletic player, there's been many a great dribbler, there's been many a good goalscorer, but not many of them have played for Bayern Munich," Herdman said. "And not many of them have won a Champions League at the age of 20 and a [Northern Star Award] and has got my daughter following him on TikTok. You know? This is what's changed."

Davies's story is far from over.

He could stay at Bayern Munich for the rest of his career and become a club legend — already, technical director Marco Neppe sees him as "one of the faces" of the team. He could try his hand at one of Europe's other top competitions, such as the English Premier League. He could return to Canada and finish his career where it all began. Or, who knows, he could decide to retire after the 2026 World Cup and become an actor.

"I think he has the opportunity to do whatever he wants with the sport now and really create a legacy," Dalrymple said.

There are many ways this could go from here, but one thing's for sure: he's already left an indelible mark on the sport in Canada.

No matter what comes next.

"I'm happy that I can wear the Canadian jersey with pride and I'm happy that I can say that I'm a Canadian playing overseas doing well," Davies said in 2020. "I just want to inspire the next generation of Canadian players to do the same. Players that are coming through the ranks right now, young players, that are trying to make it.

"I just want to give them a little light of hope."

Davies has accomplished a lot in his young life.

He'd won 12 trophies with Bayern Munich by age 21, not to mention his never-ending list of individual accolades. Updating the "honours" section of his Wikipedia page must be a full-time job. Most players can only dream of such a trophy haul over their entire careers.

But as much as he's a soccer player, Davies has become a symbol.

He's the living, breathing example of "what can happen when refugees are given the opportunity to pursue their dreams," as he once wrote in an Instagram post celebrating World Refugee Day. And it's a responsibility he doesn't take lightly.

"Anything is possible," Davies said when asked what he wants people to take away from his story. "Don't let a label or a story hold you back in life . . . Refugees deserve to be respected as well. We are normal people. We deserve to be given a fair and equal chance . . . and when you give people those chances, they can do amazing things."

It would have been easy for Davies to ignore or downplay his refugee background. After all, he doesn't have memories from his time in Buduburam. But instead he decided to embrace it. He's seen all the messages. He's spoken to other refugees.

He knows there are a lot of people that look up to him.

"I believe my personal story can help make a difference in people's lives," Davies told a roundtable of journalists following his appointment as a UNHCR global goodwill ambassador in March 2021.

The UNHCR doesn't just hand out that title to anyone. Davies was the first soccer player and first Canadian to earn the honour.

It just felt right.

Remember, this was the same organization that gave his family a home when they had nowhere else to go — his parents still have his UNHCR registration card issued in Buduburam when he was a toddler. The same organization that ultimately helped them find a new one in Canada. At its very core, the UNHCR's mandate is to save lives and build a better future for refugees and others who have been forced to flee.

People like Davies.

He knows that he probably wouldn't be here today without the support the UNHCR provided. He doesn't know where he'd be. So when the opportunity to work with them presented itself, it was something he genuinely wanted to be a part of.

"He's still very proud of it," Khimji said. "He even says his greatest accomplishment outside of soccer is when he was appointed a UNHCR goodwill ambassador."

For Davies, it's all about giving back.

There's no remuneration. Not a dime. His main role is to help raise awareness and funds around the UNHCR's work and promote access to sport and education, the things closest to him and his family. They've already discussed plans to build and renovate soccer fields and schools in refugee camps and across Africa, for example. It's not just a feel-good story.

They truly want to make a difference.

"The goal is, once everything is ready, to get Alphonso to go back home for the first time," Khimji said. "That's something he really wants to do."

For a long time, athletes have been told to "stick to sports" and stay away from commenting on social issues. Just ask Colin Kaepernick, who was chastised for kneeling during the U.S. national anthem in protest of racial inequality. Or LeBron James, who was infamously told to "shut up and dribble."

But Davies is a part of a new generation of athletes that's not afraid to stand up for what they believe in. Whether that's shining a light on the needs and success stories of refugees, supporting the Black Lives Matter movement, or raising money for various humanitarian relief efforts, Davies understands he has a platform. He understands he has a voice.

"And he understands that he can use that for the right reasons," Khimji said.

This is a reflection of his own values, and they're shared by his inner circle.

His agency is made up of staff and clients who come from different immigrant and refugee backgrounds themselves. Huoseh, the founder, is the son of a Palestinian refugee. And Khimji tells the story of his mother having to flee her home in Zanzibar overnight on a small dinghy before eventually immigrating to Canada.

These are people Davies has known for years. They are people he trusts.

As an agency, they've made a conscious effort to speak out against injustices and help vulnerable communities, and it's something they fully support Davies doing as well. Even when it's not always popular. That's the other side to all this that can't be ignored.

The ugly side.

"You'd be surprised the things we hear from people in his DMs," Khimji said. "You get people calling him the N-word, spewing racial hate at him for supporting Black Lives Matter. I remember when he spoke about Palestine, those were probably some of the worst DMs I've ever seen in his message requests. Not even just like you're a loser or you're an N-word. It's like, you're an N-word and I hope this happens to your mom and your dad. I hope one day you get chopped up. Just some really violent, gory stuff."

Khimji said that Davies is usually able to brush off any of the hateful, racist messages he receives. Sadly, as a Black man, he's seen a lot of them. But one time felt "different." And it came from a simple picture that Jordyn Huitema posted of the couple posing together on vacation in Spain. Before long, her comment section and their respective inboxes were flooded with derogatory messages condemning their interracial relationship.

"For him, he knows how to shut it off," Khimji said. "Now he's trying to teach her how to deal with it . . . That one hit a bit harder, because Jordyn was targeted and affected as well."

It hasn't always been easy, but through it all, Davies has remained steadfast in his values and beliefs. After that particular incident, he and Huitema didn't go into hiding. Instead, they called out the "disgusting" messages they'd received and posted close-up photos of each other, creating an impromptu anti-racism campaign that was amplified by various organizations and individuals around the world.

Davies doesn't want to stick to sports. Why should he?

His story is so much bigger than that.

"He has a true meaning of 'I know where I come from, I know how lucky I am,'" said Carl Valentine, a fellow Black immigrant who made Canada home. "While he's on this earth and he's doing what he's doing, he's going to affect as many lives as he can. You can see he wants to affect change. And that's pretty powerful for someone so young."

On the eve of the Tokyo 2020 Paralympic Games, Davies worked with the UNHCR to release an open letter to six refugees participating in the competition as part of the Refugee Paralympic Team. He congratulated them on the accomplishment, offered some words of encouragement, and eloquently described the impact they were about to make. He was talking about the Paralympians, of course, but he could have very easily been describing his own story.

"You are all role models now with the power to inspire others," he wrote. "Make no mistake, what you are about to do in Tokyo will change people's lives. There are going to be young people who will take up sport because of you. There will be refugees who, through watching you succeed, will believe they can too. And you know what, those people are the next nurses, teachers, and scientists. That's change starting with sport."

That's the Davies effect.

CHAPTER 17:
HUMBLE BEGINNINGS

His career had taken off at Bayern Munich. He was making millions of dollars. And finally, *finally*, Davies was able to tell his parents that they didn't need to work anymore.

One problem: they liked working. It was part of their DNA.

They didn't want to stop living their lives.

"While he was winning the Champions League, his mom was working night shifts cleaning up schools and universities," Kassim Khimji said. "And his dad was still working at the butchery farm."

It took some arm-twisting, but after a while, they reluctantly agreed to take a break.

All Davies ever wanted to do was take care of his parents. So, when he got to talking with Huoseh about their future, he was eager to help in any way possible.

"Since we came to Canada, my parents have worked very hard and have sacrificed a lot," Davies said. "I just want to give them a better life, so they don't have to worry about anything."

Davies's goal wasn't necessarily to win the Champions League and become one of the best soccer players in the world — that was a dream.

It was to buy his parents a house and a new car.

It's what he told the Manchester United scout at age 15 when they first met in Vancouver, it's what he told his high school

208

cooking teacher when they got to talking about his aspirations in life, and it's one of the first things he told Huoseh after the move to Bayern.

"I asked his family, 'What do you guys like?' Huoseh recalled. "They said, 'We like your house, Nick. Can you build one like it?' So I kind of mimicked mine, but just made his a little bit bigger. He pretty much paid for the whole thing. He helped his family out quite a bit."

His *whole* family.

For a while, Davies's mom had been driving his first car. She was happy to. But on one trip home, he surprised her with a new one. And then he gave the old one to his big sister, whose family now lives in the duplex Davies's parents had previously saved up to buy.

Their new home is just down the street from Huoseh on some acreages outside of Edmonton, rather than in the city itself.

That was partly by design.

"His mom says, 'Before Alphonso, no one in the community wanted to know me and now everyone wants to come close to me,'" Khimji said. "So they put the house in the middle of nowhere."

Davies's parents are private people. Always have been. They're not going to change now.

And neither is he.

Whenever Davies is back in Edmonton, he spends most of his time with family. After caring for his younger siblings every single day growing up, he's missed a lot of their lives ever since leaving home. So he tries to soak it in at any given opportunity.

"You can see a very special connection there with his brother," Talal Al-Awaid said. "You can see the way his brother looks up to him. They're almost joined at the hip when Alphonso's in town. Even when he's hanging out with his friends, his younger brother is around."

If Davies isn't with family during his holidays, he's usually hanging out with the same friends he's always had — his day ones, his squad. They play pool in his basement, go out for dinner at Cactus Club or Joey's, hit up the local soccer fields to watch their friends play, and, of course, drop in at West Edmonton Mall for some shopping and ice skating.

He doesn't like it when his friends draw extra attention towards him.

In fact, he's specifically asked them not to.

"When we'll go out and eat, he doesn't want his friends to say, 'Oh, this is Alphonso Davies,'" said his old friend Chernoh Fahnbulleh. "If they know him, they know him. If they don't, don't put out his name like that and say he's famous, blah, blah, blah. So what if he's famous? He's just the same dude from back then. He doesn't want people to think differently of him, just because now he's playing for a big club."

Fahnbulleh said that Davies will often foot the bill whenever he's out with friends. One night, they went paintballing with a large group. Fahnbulleh was at the front of the line, about to pay for himself, when Davies jumped in and asked how much it'd cost to pay for everyone.

"Alright, I'll cover it," he remembered Davies saying.

He's also helped out a lot at Edmonton's BTB Soccer Academy through the years, covering the costs for hundreds of soccer balls and jerseys. One winter, they were having a charity event around Christmas and Davies showed up with a bag full of game-worn, autographed Bayern Munich jerseys to auction off.

Davies is an official ambassador for the academy, but he was never asked for any monetary or material contribution. That was done on his own accord.

"He reached out one day and said, 'What can I help you guys with? How can I give back?'" Al-Awaid recalled.

All that money has gone back into the program to help the kids, Al-Awaid said, including nearly half of them that come from lower-income families.

"It's the support that he provides that helps get some of these kids going," he continued. "Not having to buy soccer balls for our program over the last couple years, not having to buy training kits, really helps us focus on putting money back into the program, to be able to run it and bring in proper coaches. He's never stopped doing that."

Davies has remained loyal to the people who helped him along the way. People like Huoseh, who is still his agent despite advances from others. And he's always happy to give back to his community.

In the summer of 2022, he committed to a three-hour meet-and-greet at an Edmonton burger joint to help raise money for the Stollery Children's Hospital. But he ended up staying for seven hours so everyone who'd been waiting could get an autograph. The event raised close to $11,000 for the hospital, including a donation from Davies himself.

A few months later, he announced that he'd be donating his earnings from the 2022 FIFA World Cup to charity, citing his desire to give back to the country that gave his family "the opportunity for a better life" and "enabled [him] to live [his] dreams."

Davies isn't afraid to spend money on others, or even himself.

A self-proclaimed "sneakerhead," as he told GQ Sports in a video about his 10 essential items, Davies owns hundreds of sneakers, for example. In his old Munich apartment, he had an entire room dedicated to his sneaker collection. He called it his "prized possession," while doing a house tour on his YouTube vlog. He also owns a few luxury watches, which he included among his essential items in the GQ Sports video.

At the same time, he won't just throw his money away on anything. He's not wired that way.

There was one time, after he'd made the move to Bayern, that he simply refused to pay a three-dollar charge to withdraw money from a different bank's ATM.

"So we drove around for like 30 or 40 minutes looking for, I think it was a BMO at the time, because he didn't want to pay the three-dollar fee," Fahnbulleh laughed. "We're like, 'Bro, come on.' He's like, 'No, I'm going to find this ATM.'"

It was a matter of principle.

Though he doesn't like to "show off," Khimji said, Davies clearly isn't trying to hide anything, either. And from his perspective, it all comes down to one thing. It's the same reason he spends hours on Twitch playing video games and interacting with fans. The same reason he makes music. And the same reason he once joined a group of star-struck locals for a pickup soccer game while vacationing in Malta.

"I do my best to enjoy life," Davies said. "People will always have their opinions, good or bad. I just try to do what brings me happiness and people around me happiness, and I focus on that."

While it's easy to get wrapped up in Davies the soccer player, or Davies the symbol, it's Davies the human being that his parents always worried about. They didn't want him to fall down the wrong path, to become a "bad boy."

Davies didn't have a normal childhood, by any stretch of the imagination. In a conversation with Huoseh a few years after moving to Germany, he said he still wanted to get his high school degree — which he never managed to complete in Vancouver — and "try a real job" for at least a couple of days.

"He goes, 'All my friends had real jobs. I've never worked a real job in my life,'" Huoseh recalled. "I think he feels like he missed out on something in life."

The life of a professional athlete, the life of a celebrity, heck, the life of a teenager, each comes with a lot of pressures that tend to manifest at one point or another. And from age 15, Davies was living all three of those lives at the same time. That's a lot to deal with.

For some, it can be too much.

Davies isn't perfect. Nor should anyone expect him to be. There have been, and will be, missteps. But he's surrounded himself with good people who have his best interests at heart. He's found release valves along the way. And he's never forgotten where he came from.

He's not where he is today despite his humble beginnings. It's because of them.

They've shaped the way he lives his life every single day.

When Davies left home at age 14, he promised his parents that he wasn't going to change. He was going to be the same person. He was going to make them proud.

They were terrified to let him go, but they trusted and believed in their son.

And he's still trying to keep that promise.

"I want to make my parents proud not because I am a good athlete, but because I am a good person," Davies said. "That's always my goal every day."

EPILOGUE

A country collectively held its breath.

In just two-and-a-half weeks, Canada would be playing their first game at the 2022 FIFA World Cup. That's it. Eighteen days before the Canadian men's national team returned to the beautiful game's biggest stage. After 36 years, the wait was almost over.

But for now, Davies had some final business to take care of with his club. On this Saturday afternoon in the German capital, he was in the lineup as Bayern Munich faced Hertha Berlin in their third-to-last game before the World Cup break.

It was unusual for teams to be playing so close to the World Cup. But with this one taking place in Qatar, the decision was made to avoid the sweltering summer heat and instead hold the competition in November and December — right smack in the middle of the European soccer season. This led to many players agonizingly missing the World Cup with injuries. Players like Paul Pogba, N'Golo Kanté, and Davies's Bayern teammate Sadio Mané, to name a few.

Suddenly, it appeared Davies may be added to that list, as he pulled up from a sprint in the 64th minute, grimacing and grabbing his right hamstring. With Davies doubled over, the referee approached him and immediately motioned for a substitution. Flanked by two of Bayern's trainers, he limped off the field with a look of consternation that was shared from coast-to-coast in Canada.

"Oh my gosh," Canadian MMA journalist Ariel Helwani tweeted to his 1.2 million followers. "Our worst nightmare."

"Best case scenario, nothing there," OneSoccer and CBC Sports host Andi Petrillo tweeted. "Bad scenario, it's a strain and it becomes a race against the clock for World Cup. Worst case scenario, hamstring is torn and he's out."

John Herdman, who was watching the game from Bahrain ahead of Canada's World Cup tune-up camp, sent Davies a message on WhatsApp to check in right away. And within 30 minutes of Davies leaving the field, he was on a group call with his national team medical staff.

"It was a scary moment for everyone," Herdman said.

Many feared the worst. And that was exacerbated when Bayern head coach Julian Nagelsmann revealed after the game that Davies had torn at least one muscle fibre, which some observers misunderstood to be a complete tear.

In reality, no one quite knew the severity, including Davies himself, until the next morning, when medical scans revealed that he'd only suffered a strain. And most importantly, as Bayern stated rather definitively, that his participation in the World Cup was "not at risk."

Still, Davies's status dominated the discussion leading up to Canada's first game. When the national team convened in Qatar and held their first full training session, Davies was noticeably absent. He was still in Munich rehabbing under the watchful eye of Bayern's medical staff, who specifically stayed in town to care for him. That led to further speculation, but Herdman felt it gave Davies the best chance to heal at the fastest rate possible.

"It's a Ferrari, an F1 car, in a Ferrari garage," he told his staff, referencing the world-class resources at Bayern's disposal. "You wouldn't move that car into a different garage to start a repair and healing process. It just didn't make sense."

Davies would remain in Munich for most of the week before touching down in Qatar the night of November 18, five days before Canada's first game against Belgium.

"I'm ready," he told a Canada Soccer staffer upon his arrival at the team hotel in Lusail — a sentiment he reiterated to TSN's James Duthie in an interview that aired before the tournament opener between Qatar and Ecuador.

Herdman played it coy when he met with the media, cautioning that Davies hadn't yet pushed his hamstring to its limits. That part was true — they weren't going to put him through his max speed test until two days before the game. But Herdman later admitted that he also wanted to keep Belgium guessing and not give away too much too soon.

In the back of his mind, he could sense Davies was ready.

"My mission is to make sure he plays at this World Cup," Herdman said.

Once again, a country collectively held its breath.

There was no debate. No discussion. Once the referee pointed towards the spot, awarding Canada a penalty kick, Davies picked up the ball without hesitation.

"I have faith in myself, and my teammates have faith in me," he later said, having officially been cleared to start. "So, I stepped up to the plate."

Twelve yards in front of him, Davies saw the imposing figure of 6-foot-7 goalkeeper Thibaut Courtois bouncing from side to side on his goal line. Courtois, one of the great shot-stoppers of the generation, was the only thing standing between the Canadian men's national team and their first-ever goal at the FIFA World Cup.

Back in Canada, more than 3.5 million viewers were glued to the game at schools, workplaces, and watch parties across the country, including inside the gymnasium of Davies's old junior high school in Edmonton. Less than 10 minutes into their first men's World Cup game since 1986, Canada was on the verge of history.

"The expectations of a nation on his shoulders," TSN commentator Luke Wileman proclaimed as Davies stood over the ball.

The referee blew his whistle. Davies took a deep breath, leaned in, and began his approach. Just like his two previous penalties for Canada, both of which he scored on, Davies side-footed the ball towards the bottom left quadrant of the goal.

Only this time, it didn't go in.

Having done his homework on Davies, Courtois dove the same direction and made the save. Davies buried his face in his palms after he and Jonathan David failed to convert on the rebound. Despite an inspired performance against a Belgian team who came into the tournament ranked second in the world, Canada lost the game 1–0.

"I'm proud of Phonzie," Herdman told the media, confirming he let the players on the field decide who'd take the penalty. "I mean, he's picked the ball up. It's a big moment for any player to do that. You're carrying the weight of a nation, 36 years of waiting, longer than 36 for the first goal. So, really proud that he picked the ball up. It takes a special character."

Prior to that game, Davies was included in the team's leadership group for the first time. He sat in on meetings with captain Atiba Hutchinson and other senior players, where they all shared some of the hardships they had to endure and some of the heroes who inspired them to get to this point. So, when Davies picked up that ball, Herdman saw a player who was "embracing leadership" and "taking responsibility in a real big moment."

"People will have their own views and opinions," he said. "But when you live it, when you're in there, when you understand what's motivating guys, what's driving them, some of the experiences they're having in the build-up to the game, yeah, I would say I was really impressed with his contribution in that space."

Davies looked dejected post-game, both on the field and in interviews. When asked by TSN sideline reporter Daniel Zakrzewski how much he was raring to go for the next game, he started his answer with: "It's tough, it's tough." Most of all, he was upset that Canada didn't get any points out of the game. In a later press conference, he said that he tried not to lose any sleep over the missed penalty but couldn't help but replay it in his mind.

"Missed penalty now part of Alphonso Davies' World Cup legacy with Canada," a *Toronto Star* headline read following the game. "But legacies can change."

And Davies's changed in a hurry.

After watching Lionel Messi and Kylian Mbappé score for their countries a day earlier, Herdman pulled Davies aside in the locker room before Canada's second game against Croatia.

"Big players arrive in big moments at tournaments," Herdman told him. "This is it. It's time. There's only a certain amount of players that can take these moments.

"And you're one of them."

Just 67 seconds into the game, Davies delivered *the moment* and etched his name into the Canadian soccer history books — as if it wasn't already engraved in stone.

Goalkeeper Milan Borjan started the sequence with a long ball that landed at the feet of Cyle Larin just beyond the halfway line. Larin brought it down with a lovely first touch, before playing it out wide to Tajon Buchanan. Davies, meanwhile, had been running towards the goal from inside his own half, watching the play develop. He accelerated right as Buchanan dropped his head and sent a mouth-watering cross towards the back post.

Thump.

Davies cruised past the nearest Croatian defender, soared into the air, and completed his 60-yard-run with a thunderous header from inside the box.

No one was saving this one.

Khalifa International Stadium erupted as the ball bounced off the pitch and flew into the back netting. Davies ran to the corner flag in a state of pure ecstasy, screaming and glancing over at the mob of his Canadian teammates who were approaching from the sideline, before taking another a giant leap and punching the air emphatically.

"That feeling will stick to me forever," Davies said in a Canada Soccer video.

From their first meeting with Herdman back in 2018, this team was on a mission to make history and inspire a new generation of Canadian soccer players. Every camp they went into, they wanted to break a record. They wanted to be pioneers, which is why Herdman had Chris Hadfield — the first Canadian astronaut to walk in space — speak to the team in Qatar. To *really* do that, they knew that participating in the World Cup wasn't enough. At the very least, they had to do what Canada's '86 World Cup team couldn't: score.

"And who else deserves it more than our guy Alphonso Davies?" Canadian midfielder Jonathan Osorio told TSN's Matthew Scianitti after the game.

It had been a challenging year for Davies, from his heart condition to his hamstring injury, and, of course, the missed penalty, but he found a way to persevere.

"He's a winner," Herdman said.

Canada ended up losing 4–1, however, and then 2–1 to Morocco in their final game. As the face of the program — his face was literally plastered on a skyscraper in downtown Doha and on the cover of *Maclean's* leading up to the tournament — Davies shouldered some of the criticism. He drew the ire of some Canadian reporters for only speaking to the rights-holding broadcasters, the likes of TSN, RDS, and beIN Sports, and not the wider media after each of the three games. Others took aim at his on-field performance, suggesting he tried to do too much and should have never taken the penalty kick against Belgium.

Ultimately, this was all part of the learning curve for Davies, who'd just turned 22 before the tournament and will still only be 25 when Canada co-hosts the 2026 FIFA World Cup. For the first time, he was truly the centre of attention in Canada. Everywhere you looked, there he was. That came with a new level of scrutiny he hadn't experienced before, and one Herdman hopes he won't ever have to again as Canada strives to produce more players like him.

"He had to carry a lot," Herdman said.

After the final whistle against Morocco, a heartbroken Davies crouched down to the pitch and covered his face. Teammate Stephen Eustáquio came over to console him, burying his head into Davies's back while gripping him tightly. Davies took some time to compose himself, then went into the crowd to embrace his parents. He hugged his mom first, and then his dad.

"We tried our best," Davies said as he wrapped his arms around their shoulders.

His parents barely got to watch him play as a kid. As they told him after the first game, they were proud of him no matter what. And judging from the overwhelming support he continued to receive from the Canadian public, so was the rest of the country.

On top of everything he'd already done for the sport, and every-thing he represented as a refugee who came to Canada for a better life and embraced the country with every ounce of his being, Davies gave Canadian soccer fans the moment they'd been longing for.

Finally, the country could exhale.

ACKNOWLEDGEMENTS

I apologize in advance for this sounding like an Oscars acceptance speech, but each individual listed below — and many others that I'm surely missing — deserves to be, well, acknowledged for the invaluable role they played in bringing this book to life.

First off, I have to thank Alphonso and his parents, Debeah and Victoria. Back in 2017, when I was still working for the Vancouver Whitecaps, you welcomed me into your home and shared your story for the first time. I tried my best to do it justice then. I hope I've done the same now.

Thank you to Alphonso's agency — in particular, Kassim Khimji and Nedal Huoseh — for putting up with all my requests. With this being an independent project, you didn't have to help me. But you did. And for that, I'll forever be grateful.

There are way too many people to name individually, but thank you to all of Alphonso's friends, teammates, coaches, teachers, and everyone else who agreed to be interviewed. It's your insights and stories — certainly not mine — that served as the foundation for this book.

Thank you to Canada Soccer, Bayern Munich, and the Vancouver Whitecaps for setting up interviews and being so accommodating through this process.

Thank you to my editor, Michael Holmes, and all the hardworking staff at ECW Press for believing in this book and for the amount of care that you put into every detail.

Thank you to my good friends, Raheem and SJ, for sending me a calendar invite to ensure I started working on a book proposal when I first mentioned this idea to you in 2018, and to all my other friends and contacts who have been so eager to help along the way.

Thank you to my brother, Shaheed, for all your advice, encouragement, and marketing support, and to the rest of my family, Azee, Bob, Sheeba, Ayden, and Zayn, for always having my back.

Finally, a big thank you to my wife, Sarah. When I needed a fresh set of eyes, you grabbed your glasses. When I needed to vent, you sat back and listened. And most importantly, when I wasn't sure if I could do this, you encouraged me to follow my passions and dreams. No questions asked. None of this would have been possible without you.